SORTED!

Evolution, nature and stuff

Glenn Murphy received his master's degree in science communication from London's Imperial College of Science, Technology and Medicine. He wrote his first popular science book, *Why Is Snot Green?*, while managing the Explainer team at the Science Museum in London. In 2007 he moved to the United States. He now lives and works in Raleigh, North Carolina, with his wife, Heather, and two unusually large and ill-tempered cats.

Favourite science fact: the eye of a colossal squid measures 27 cm (almost a foot) across. It has the largest eyes of any animal in the world.

Glenn is currently writing his ninth book.

Also by Glenn Murphy and published in association with the Science Museum

WHY IS SNOT GREEN?
and other extremely important questions (and answers) from the Science Museum

HOW LOUD CAN YOU BURP?
and other extremely important questions (and answers) from the Science Museum

STUFF THAT SCARES YOUR PANTS OFF!
The Science Museum Book of Scary Things (and ways to avoid them)

SCIENCE: SORTED!
Space, Black Holes and Stuff

SCIENCE SORTED

Evolution, nature and stuff

By Glenn Murphy

Illustrated by Mike Phillips

MACMILLAN CHILDREN'S BOOKS

This book is produced in association with the Science Museum. Royalties from the sale of this product help fund the museum's exhibitions and programmes.

The Science Museum, London Internationally recognized as one of the world's leading science centres. It contains more than 10,000 amazing exhibits, two fantastic simulator rides and the astounding IMAX cinema. Enter a world of discovery and achievement, where you can see, touch and experience real objects and icons which have shaped the world we live in today or visit www.sciencemuseum.org.uk to find out more.

First published 2010 by Macmillan Children's Books
a division of Macmillan Publishers Limited
20 New Wharf Road, London N1 9RR
Basingstoke and Oxford
Associated companies throughout the world
www.panmacmillan.com

ISBN 978-0-330-50894-0

1 3 5 7 9 8 6 4 2

A CIP catalogue record for this book is available from the British Library.

Printed and bound in the UK by CPI Mackays, Chatham ME5 8TD

To Stu Sharp and Sarah Burthe – out there in the trenches with the seabirds and meerkats . . . while I stay snug at home writing about it

Thanks to:

Gaby Morgan – in short, you rule.

Prof. Alun Williams, University of Cambridge, Department of Veterinary Medicine for his wonderfully insightful comments and suggestions. This book is all the better for your efforts.

Deborah Bloxam, Tom Vine, Deborah Jones and everyone else still kickin' it at the Science Museum.

The SCONCs – keeping me on the scientific straight and narrow since 2007.

Vladimir Vasiliev, Kwan Lee, Emmanuel Manolakakis and everyone else in the Systema community who has helped with my continuing evolution.

My lovely Heather – doing some evolving of her own this year.

Ka-ge and Austin – my fuzzy management team and constant writing companions.

As always, the Murphys and the Wittmayers.

And all our friends far and wide who make being a modern day *Homo sapiens* so much fun.

Contents

1.

What's Life All About?

[illegible]

1.
What's Life All About?

Oooh. That's a biggie! Not sure I can answer that. Come to think of it, I'm not sure I even have that one figured out myself yet . . .

Hold on – I didn't mean *that*. I mean, you know, life and living things. Life's supposed to be about evolution, and living things evolve, right? But what makes something *alive* in the first place? What actually *is* life?

Ahh – now that's a good question. That's one we can tackle. But, to be honest, it's going to take a whole book to do it, and we'll have to explore every nook and cranny of the living world to figure it out.

We'll be sticking bacteria and bugs under the microscope. We'll be diving into the deepest oceans to prod at starfish, sponges and jellyfish. We'll sail the world with Charles Darwin, and see how birds, barnacles and sea-dragons led him to his famous theory of evolution. We'll leap with lizards, fly with bats and birds, scuttle with spiders, slither with snakes, and hunt with dangerous carnivores.

Along the way, we'll find out how to name and recognize animals, just as zoologists do. We'll see how animals adapt to changing environments and deadly predators. We'll discover the links between dolphins, dingoes and dinosaurs. And we'll have some *serious fun*.

Have fun? I thought this was a *science* book . . .
It is. But, believe it or not, science can be amazing, spectacular, brilliant fun. If you've read one of my other books, like *Why Is Snot Green?* or *How Loud Can You Burp?*, you'll have seen tonnes of fun, science-y stuff already. You wouldn't believe how much fun stuff there really is. All we're going to do differently here is tackle the science one subject at a time. But that doesn't mean we're skipping on the fun. Far from it. Aside from all the crazy facts and fascinating theories, there are puzzles, quizzes, experiments and more.

Now where were we? Oh yeah – **life**.

2.
Life on Earth

Life, in some ways, is still a mystery. We know that life on Earth began over 3.6 billion years ago, a little more than a billion years after the planet itself was formed.

It took a wee while to get started, then?
Right. But once it did it was off like the clappers.

What do you mean?
Well, we know that life began with simple, microscopic creatures no more complex than a few chemicals in a fatty ball. And we know that from there life developed into everything from seaweed and sharks to trees, toadstools and tyrannosaurs. A few million years later, we had large mammals, monkeys and apes. And it wasn't too long after that the first humans hit the scene.

So life on Earth has developed from little fatty balls

floating in a murky sea to farmers, artists, architects, engineers, scientists, philosophers, presidents, politicians, pop stars and reality TV contestants.* Not bad.

Wow – that is quite a jump.

In a way, yes. But you also have to remember that the whole path from bacteria to Britney Spears took billions of years to trudge. With a couple of hundred years of *biology* – the study of life – under our belts, we're now fairly sure of how most of this came about, and how long it all took to happen. Living things evolved from simple to complex in a series of tiny steps taking millions of years each, steered by natural processes of life, death and change.

We'll be exploring all this throughout the course of this book. By the end of it all, hopefully, you'll look at the living world in a whole new way – knowing how, where and why it all came to be. But there's one more thing we need to know before we set off on our global safari: which things should we look at, and which should we skip?

Er . . . shouldn't we just look at living things, and skip the rest?

Okay. Sounds good. But what do we mean by 'living things?'

---

* Some scientists question whether this one group represents a real step forward from bacteria. I think perhaps not.

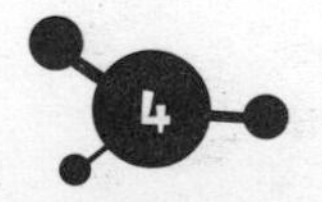

I dunno. Bacteria and plants and monkeys and stuff.
Okay . . . and 'the rest'?

Well . . . all the *other* stuff. You know, rocks . . . soil . . . islands . . . underpants. Stuff like that.
Sounds reasonable enough. But while these things are not alive in themselves many rocks and soils are positively *teeming* with life, and some islands are built entirely from living organisms. (And believe me, you don't want to know how many things are living in your underpants right now.)

Really?
Yep. Just because you can't see or recognize them right away, that doesn't mean they're not alive. Living things come in an enormously wide variety of shapes, sizes and forms, many of which were – until fairly recently – not really thought of as *alive* at all. So we can hardly set about defining life before we can all agree on *what's alive* and *what isn't*.

Oh, come on. How hard could that be?
Well, let's give it a whirl.

Look at the list of things below, and sort them into two groups – alive (A) and not alive (B). I've done the first two for you. Off you go, then.

A		B
Monkey		Rock
	Jellyfish	
	Toothbrush	
	Sponge	
	Bacteria	
	Virus	
	Tree	
	Mountain	
	River	
	Coral reef	
	Mud	
	Mould	
	Mushrooms	

All done?

Okay – let's see how many you got.

Only **six** things on the list were **not** actually living things. These were: **rock, toothbrush, virus, mountain, river** and **mud**. All the rest were alive.

***What?* Even the sponge? The coral reef? And the mould?**

Yep. While the sponge in your bathroom may not be alive, there are entire families of living sponges in the ocean. Believe it or not, they're actually animals.

Many of these sit on coral reefs – which may look

like big, undersea rock piles, but are, in fact, animals too! Or, rather, they're the joined outer bodies of thousands of reef-building animals (called polyps), closely related to jellyfish.

And the mould on your bathroom tiles (or furring up that half-eaten tub of baked beans in the fridge), well, that's alive too. It's a type of fungus – an ancient form of life that was lurking here on Earth for millions of years before we turned up.

No way! I thought living things had to . . . you know . . . *move* and *do stuff*.

Well, they all **do stuff**, but not all of them **move** that much. Think about it – most trees and plants remain stationary for life, save for a bit of upward growth. And, on the flipside, icebergs and rivers move, and no one would say that *they're* alive, right?

Err . . . right. I s'pose so. So, if living things can look like lifeless ones, how do we decide which is which?

Gooooood question. To help us out with that, biologists have come up with a list of features that all living things *must* have. A kind of 'life list'. Basically, if they have *all* these features, they're alive; if not, they're not. Simple.

So here they are:

1) **Living things self-organize**. They arrange themselves into bodies and structures. This can

be as simple as the fatty bubble surrounding the watery chemical core of a bacterium. Or as complex as the bones, guts and muscles of a racehorse. What's important is that **living things sort themselves out.**

2) **Living things reproduce**. They make copies of themselves, which in turn make copies of *them*selves, and gradually grow in number to create an entire *colony* or *species*.

3) **Living things eat stuff**. Or, rather, they absorb chemicals and minerals from their environment and turn them into either a) bits of their bodies or b) energy to power all that eating, organizing and reproducing. Most animals have to chew and digest their food using guts. But bacteria, fungi and simple animals like sponges just absorb their food through their bodies instead.

4) **Living things change things**. You know when living organisms have been around, because they alter their surroundings. Largely as a result of all that organizing, reproducing and eating . . .

5) **Living things have life-cycles**. They show predictable, programmed patterns that take them from the beginning to the end of their lives – through birth, growth, reproduction and death.

Now if you go back and look at the As and Bs in your list once more, you'll see how much easier it is to recognize the living and the non-living. Mountains may seem to grow (over time), and rivers can alter their environments by carving out canyons. But neither one of these actually eats things* or reproduces.

Corals, mushrooms and moulds may all just sit there *looking* lifeless. But in fact they all self-organize, eat, reproduce, alter their surroundings and follow repeating lifecycles.

Wow. Never thought of it like that. So what about viruses?

They're a tricky one. In a sense, they do all these things too. But most biologists don't think of them as truly alive because they cheat on #1. They don't really self-organize or self-reproduce – they squeeze into the cells of other living creatures, which do all the assembling, organizing and copying *for* them. Therefore, because they're either non-living things – or the laziest living things on the planet – we'll be skipping the viruses in our global life-safari.

So, now we know what to look for, it's time to set off and explore the planet.

Hmmmm . . . but where should we start? With so

---

* Except, perhaps, the occasional mountain climber or canoeing enthusiast.

many living things in the world, it's hard to know where to begin . . .

Couldn't we just start with antelopes and finish up with zebras?
Ahh, but then we'll only cover the animals. Plus you've already skipped aardvarks, aardwolves and anteaters.

Oh.
On the other hand, you're right – we can't just wade in there without a plan. If we're going to tackle a whole world full of living things, we need some way of sorting them all out first. Thankfully, there's a science that lets us do just that. *Zoology.*

So we're starting at the zoo, then?
In a way, yes. So grab your sunblock and a pair of good walking shoes. We're off to find out how all the animals in the zoo got their names . . .

3.
Life-ology

Who invented biology?

No one did. Biology is, literally, 'the study (or science) of life', and in a way it's almost as old as humankind itself. Humans have been watching and studying wildlife for as long as they've been around to do it, and that's part of how we came to be so successful as a species. The modern science of biology didn't begin until the seventeenth or eighteenth century, and the famous biologist Charles Darwin didn't chip in his ideas until the middle of the ninteenth. And while Darwin didn't actually invent biology, it's fair to say that his ideas changed it completely, and forever.

Hang on – how can biology be as old as humankind? That's impossible. I mean, cavemen didn't have schools and science labs, did they?
No, they didn't. But the study of life existed long before we started calling it 'biology' and sending kids to school to study it. In a sense, for as long as people have gazed upon plants, trees, animals and nature itself, there have been amateur biologists in the world.

How d'you figure that?
Well, early humans evolved in Africa around 300,000

years ago, and over the next 250,000 years they spread themselves right across the globe – throughout the Middle East, Europe, Asia, Australia and the Americas. But they only managed that through a keen understanding of the plants and animals that formed the natural world around them.

At first, our ancestors learned to recognize edible and non-edible berries, fruits, roots and mushrooms, and learned where to find fish, shellfish and small animals. Later, they observed the movements and habits of large animals, following herds on their annual migrations, and learning when, where and how to hunt them for food. Later still, they experimented with keeping wild animals and growing plants near their permanent homes – rather than hunting and scavenging for them in the wild – and a new age of **farming** was born. From there, they tamed wild dogs and cats to protect their villages and grain stores, and tamed horses to carry them across huge distances (and into furious battles).

Eventually, humans used this newfound mastery of food and free travel to conquer the entire globe. But none of this would have been possible without their knowledge of the natural world. So, in a way, we owe all our successes to those early human biologists.

Wow. Never thought about it like that. I thought biology was all just looking at plants and butterflies, and putting insects in jars and stuff.
That's part of it, certainly. But as you can see there's a lot more to it than that.

So what's all the things-in-jars stuff about, then?
The things-in-jars stuff only started a couple of hundred years ago, and actually represents quite an important turning point in the history of biology. Sometime in the nineteenth century, the study of the natural world went from being a pastime or hobby to being an official *science*.

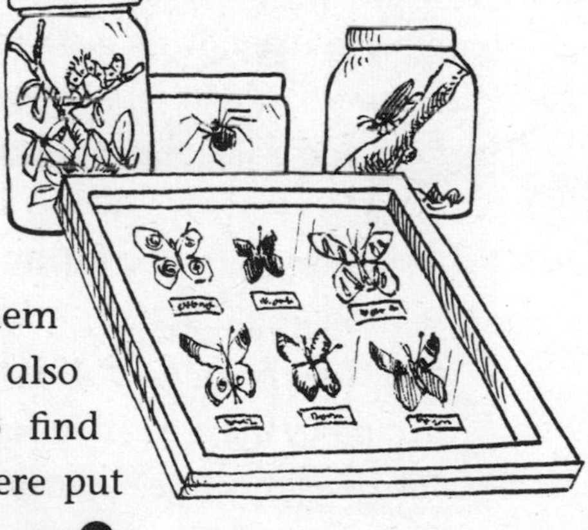

Before that, amateur collectors and observers of the living world called themselves **naturalists** or **natural philosophers**. Often wealthy, world-travelling types, they collected living things in jars, sketched them artfully in journals, and started to sort them and name them. They also cut dead things up to find out how their bodies were put together and occasionally came up with a theory for why something looked or behaved the way it did. But it was only in the nineteenth century, when the study of life became a full-time job, that the modern *science* of biology was born.

So proper biology started with rich tourists, artists and bug collectors?
Yes. Well . . . sort of.

So if I start collecting bugs and sketching plants, does that make me a proper biologist too?
Well, it'd be a good start. And if you want to have a go, try a few of the activities below.

Back-garden biology

- Pond sampling – clean out an empty jam jar and use it to scoop a water sample from your local pond. Then look at drops of it under a magnifying glass (or, better still, microscope) and count how many water fleas and other bugs you can see.

- Beachcombing – if you live near the seaside, visit it at low tide and find three or more rockpools left behind by the retreating waves. Turn over rocks, peer beneath,

and see how many different types of crabs and shellfish (like limpets, whelks and mussels) you can find. Also, comb the beach for shells, crab skeletons, seaweed and shark-egg cases ('mermaid's purses'). See how many different plant and animal species you can identify from the evidence.

- Birdwatching – grab a friend or family member, a pair of binoculars and a guidebook detailing the birds in your area (preferably one with lots of pictures). Then head into a local wood, forest or meadow. See how many bird species you can spot during a one-hour walk.

But if you want to call yourself a *proper* biologist you'll have to get a bit more organized and serious about your collecting and studying. Real biology (and real science in general) is not just about looking and collecting. It's also about thinking, testing and figuring things out.

Even back in the nineteenth century, most 'naturalists' simply collected and sketched things for fun. Only a small number of them made detailed studies, came up with theories or set about naming* animal species and plant families.

* For more about this, see 'How do animals get their names?' on page 27.

Keen as they were, these early biologists were, for the most part, doing little more than scrapbooking the world. Through those early collections and observations, we learned quite a bit about *how* living things look and behave, but not much about *why* they look or behave that way.

Why not?

Because although they discovered a lot about individual plants, animals and other organisms, they didn't really understand how they *related* to each other, nor where all those different species *came from* in the first place. They couldn't come up with a single, solid theory to explain it all.

Enter Charles Darwin – and his famous *theory of evolution*. Darwin's idea about the evolution and *natural selection* of surviving species turned the whole scientific world upside down, and changed the way we look at biology, forever.

Oh, come on. How could one idea do all that?

Ahh – *that*'s another story entirely. But I'm glad you asked . . .

What's the big deal about evolution?

Charles Darwin's theory of evolution was the first scientific theory to explain the appearance and behaviour of not just ***some****, but* ***all*** *living species. It told us* ***how all living things were related****. As if that wasn't enough, it also explained the* ***origin*** *of* ***new species****, why some species become* ***extinct****, and the* ***reason*** *for the great* ***variety*** *of living species on the planet.*

Darwin really did all that at once? With *one* idea?

Yep – pretty much. Although it took him a while to come out with it. And when he eventually did, not everybody accepted it right away.*

In the end, though, there was no getting around it. The theory was so simple it was *beautiful*.

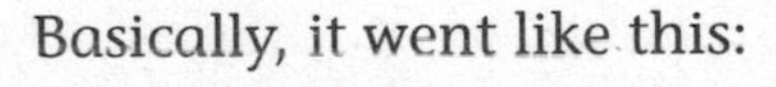

Basically, it went like this:

1. Living things, even within a species, vary in appearance and behaviour. Individual animals may be bigger or smaller, faster or slower, more

---

* And in fact, a few other naturalists besides Darwin – like Alfred Russell Wallace – were beginning to have similar thoughts at the time. More about that later on.

or less attractive, more or less intelligent. This is called *natural variation.*

2. Depending on the time and place (climate, amount of food available, number of nasty predators around, etc.), some members of this species will be better able to survive (or have more babies) than others.

3. Therefore, the animals best suited to their surroundings will have more babies, while those less well suited will either die or fail to reproduce. This is called *natural selection.*

4. Over time, this means all surviving members of a species will end up looking like those 'best suited' winners, as they will be the only ones left around. (At least until the environment changes.) This effect has been nicknamed '*survival of the fittest*'.

5. If two groups of animals from a single species are separated, and find themselves in different environments, then each group will evolve to fit its own environment – just as described above. Eventually, the two groups will become so different that they form *two separate species.* This is *how new species are created.*

That's it? That's the whole theory?

Well, no – not quite. There's a bit more to it than that. For example, the 'environment' can change in many different ways, and animal groups don't necessarily have to be physically separated (say, by mountains or rivers) in order to form new species. Sometimes a change in depth, diet, weather or the habits of choosy female animals can be enough to do it. But we'll get to all that later on.

The point is this one idea made sense of all the random observations and ideas that had come before it. It was as if the 'big book of biology' was written in Japanese,* and suddenly Darwin lobbed us an English-Japanese dictionary.

That's a pretty impressive trick. So how did Darwin come up with the idea in the first place? Did he just dream it up one day?

Actually, Darwin didn't really come up with the idea of evolution himself. It had been around for quite a few years beforehand. Nor, as some of the history books say, did he come up with the whole idea during his famous round-the-world voyage on board the *Beagle* (if you haven't heard about that, don't worry – there's more on that in a minute).

Instead, he figured it out gradually, over many

* Or, for Japanese readers, Swahili or something. You get what I mean.

years, and kept his ideas to himself. Only when someone else threatened to beat him to the finish-line did he write his famous book . . . which changed the face of science forever.

He sailed around the world? What for?

From December 1831 to October 1836, Darwin sailed right around the world on board a ship called the *Beagle* – invited as a 'gentleman companion' for the ship's map-making captain, Robert FitzRoy. But he later appointed himself **ship's naturalist** and began sending samples of the plants, animals and fossils he found back to London for later study.

On his way around the coast of South America, Darwin found some mysterious fossils in Argentina. These turned out to be **giant ground sloths** (see above) and **American camels** that had long since become extinct. Later, he discovered a tiny, endangered species of South American ostrich called a **rhea** (see left).

Actually, he and the captain unknowingly *ate* one, after locals captured and cooked it.

Darwin *ate* an endangered species? That wasn't too cool!

Yep. Actually, that particular species is now extinct,* partly thanks to the crew of the *Beagle*. And that wasn't the only endangered species Darwin and the captain ate on that trip. Still, being a good scientist (if not a great conservationist), Darwin kept the bones and sent them to London anyway.

Through all this, he took notes in which he wondered about the plight of extinct animals. Where had they all gone? Had the locals eaten them all? Why did some species survive, while others disappeared? At the time, most naturalists thought that God had created every species on Earth, exactly as it was, purely to feed, entertain and serve mankind. But why, Darwin thought, would He create a species just to let it be destroyed? Hmm . . .

Is that what gave him the idea of natural selection and stuff?

No, not quite. But it did start him thinking. And he continued his biological detective work throughout the entire voyage.

Later in the trip, Darwin trekked through the rainforests of Peru and was dumbstruck by the huge variety of plants, trees, birds, insects, monkeys and

---

* Thankfully, two other rhea species managed to avoid being eaten to extinction, and still survive today.

other animals on display. Again he wondered: if all these species were there for Man's benefit, why would God create such a huge number of them, and then stick them in such a remote place, so far out of sight?

***Now* did he get it?**

Nope. Not yet. A few weeks later, on its way west across the Pacific Ocean, the *Beagle* landed briefly on an isolated set of islands 600 miles (1,000 km) west of Ecuador, known as the **Galapagos Islands**. Here, too, Darwin discovered an incredible variety of animal life, including giant, lumbering tortoises and scary-looking marine iguanas – perched like dragons or dinosaurs on rocks near the shore. Again he wondered: why such a rich variety of animal life, so far from human eyes?

Among these many species, Darwin also sketched, collected and labelled dozens of bird species previously unknown to naturalists. He sent them back to a friend in London to identify them – labelling them, as best he knew, as finches, wrens, thrushes and woodpeckers. At the time, he didn't recognize the importance of these birds to his theory. But years later, once he was happily back in England with his family, Darwin's bird-expert friend told him that they were all, in fact, types of finch – now known as **Galapagos finches**. They just *looked* like other bird families because of their different body sizes and beak shapes.

But why, Darwin thought, would there be so many different species of finch in one place? With this, Darwin realized that each species of finch had adapted (or changed) in order to eat a different diet – eating either seeds, nuts, insects, fruit or cactuses found on the island. Finches with parrot-like beaks cracked nuts, while those with thin, woodpecker-like beaks probed trees for insects, and so on. The birds with beaks best suited to the local food sources had survived and reproduced, while those with less ideal beak shapes had died off – leaving a range of different finch species that had *evolved* from a single 'ancestor'.

Small tree finches

Vegetarian finch

Cactus finches

Warbler finches

Finally! So then he told everyone all about it, right?

Nope. He went home. He waited. He studied other living things – like barnacles, orchids and domestic dog breeds – that made him think again and again about his theory. And he continued to compile notes and write essays for himself. But he never spoke openly about his ideas, much less published them. Not for over two decades.

***What?* Arrghhhh! Why not?**

Partly because he knew that the idea of evolution would be thought of as ridiculous, or even *dangerous*, and he feared for his reputation. You have to remember that almost everybody, at that time, thought that God had created all living things at once, and placed them perfectly throughout the world. Darwin knew that some people would think it was blasphemy (or insulting to God and the church) to say otherwise. So he waited and waited – collecting facts and making notes to himself. For over twenty years.

Sigh. So when did he finally come out with it?

In 1858, when a younger man named Alfred Russell Wallace wrote to him, telling him of his own theories of evolution. Inspired by the travel tales of Darwin and other naturalists, Wallace embarked on his own round-the-world journey via Brazil and, later, Malaysia. There, he noticed the similarities between two classes of mammals* separated by the geography of the islands. From this, he deduced – much as Darwin did with his finches – that even quite different mammal species would develop to look like each other if their environments and needs were very similar. Darwin panicked, thinking Wallace would beat him to the punch, got his many decades' worth of notes together and published as soon as he could. The book – *On the Origin of Species* – became one of the most famous, influential and controversial books of all time.

Whoa. I knew evolution was supposed to be important and stuff. But I didn't realize it was *that* big a deal.

It really was. And it still is.

In fact, it's been said that 'nothing in biology makes sense *except* in the light of evolution'. Before Darwin's theory, our ideas about where the huge variety of living species on Earth came from were, at best, wild stabs in the dark. At worst, they were myths or mistakes.

But now we know *everything* about how life works, right?

No, not at all. There's still a great deal that we don't understand. But thanks to Darwin we know a *lot*

---

* In particular, between the mammals found from Borneo northwards, and the *marsupials* found further south. More about these two types of mammals in Chapter 5.

more than we did. And as for the rest, we can now make more educated (and hopefully more accurate) guesses.

That's pretty good going, I s'pose.

Yep – not bad at all. Nice one, Charlie!

How do animals get their names?

Every animal has at least two *names. Their common name – like 'gorilla', 'emu' and 'tiger' is often given by local people in the areas where the animals live. But they also have an official scientific name, given to them by biologists or zoologists. And it's not just* ***animal*** *species that get their own posh technical title. Plants, fungi, bacteria and all other living things get them too.*

But how did people decide what to call them in the first place? Did some African guy just point at a gorilla once and say 'gorilla' . . . and everyone agreed?

Possibly, yes. In some cases the animal's common name is very ancient, and may have been around since human tribes first began speaking and naming them. The word 'gorilla' comes from the ancient African word *gorillai*, which the people of West Africa were using as early as 480 BC, and had probably been using for thousands of years before that. Other common names describe the animal in some way in the native language. *Orang-utan*, for example, means 'old man of the forest' in Malay. And *koala*, interestingly, means 'no drink' in some Australian aboriginal tongues.

Eh? Why would they call it a 'no drink'?

Because koalas hardly ever drink water. They get all the water they need from raindrops and dewdrops on the moist leaves they eat. The clever aborigines noticed this, and named it accordingly.

So do all animal names *mean* something like that?

Not all of them. Some locals probably chose names for the animals at random, while their languages were still fairly new. And in fact many (or most) common animal names come from other foreign places. This is because explorers and scholars from distant countries often arrived and renamed animals for themselves in their own languages. Later, *these* names would spread around the world as the scholars and explorers wrote books. Then the newer foreign names would often stick – in place of the original native ones.

The English name *sloth*, for example, means 'laziness', but the native tribes of South America know the animal as a *rit* or *ritto* (meaning 'sleeper'). Similarly, *aardvark* means 'earth pig' in Afrikaans, *hippopotamus* means 'river horse' in Greek, and *giraffe* comes from the Arabic word *zirafah*, meaning 'the tallest of them all'. Many animal names, in fact, owe more to the travels of English, Dutch, Greek and Arab scholars and sailors than they do to local tribes.

What about the posh science-y name? How does an animal get one of those?

The scientific name for a species is usually given in Latin or Greek – the old-school languages of science (and learning in general). In the old days, this allowed scholars from all over the world to understand each other without learning loads of new languages. And while scientists now tend to use English or other languages instead, the habit for naming animals in Greek or Latin has stuck around. Partly because it also simplifies things when a single species has more than one common name. The American **puma**, for example, is also commonly known as the **cougar** or **mountain lion**. But zoologists don't need to argue about which name to use, since they all know it as *Felis concolor*.

The official name normally has two parts, which usually describe the physical features of the species, and/or where you can find it. But sometimes an animal may be named after the person who discovered it, or even after famous scientists and celebrities. And this goes not just for animals, but also for plants, fungi, bacteria and protists (see page 33). You name it – and it's got a double-barrelled scientific name.

For example, the official name for the polar bear is *Ursus maritimus* ('sea bear' – since it swims so well

between ice floes of the Arctic), while the American black bear is simply *Ursus americanus* ('American bear'). Hundreds of plant and animal species have been named after Charles Darwin – including *Berberis darwinii* (Darwin's Barberry) and *Rhinoderma darwinii* (Darwin's frog). For movie fans, there's a spider called *Caplonus harrisonfordi,* and a beetle named *Agra schwarzeneggeri.*

I'm sure Indiana Jones and the beefy Austrian muscleman are quite pleased with those two.

Animal anagrams

Unravel the anagrams, and translate these scientific animal names into common ones.

Scientific name	Meaning	Common name	Common name (anagram)
Spilogale poturius	'stinking, spotty weasel'	?	desk stunk top
Orcinus orca	'killer-from-hell whale'	?	leek war hill
Ursus arctos horriblis	'horrible-bear bear'	?	barry leg ziz
Macropus rufus	'red big-foot'	?	radar ken goo
Ornitor-hynchus anatinus	'duck-like, bird-snout'	?	tacky billed sud pulp
Ailuropoda melanoleuci	'black-and-white cat-foot'	?	aid gnat nap

(*answers on page 208*)

So scientists just call the animals whatever they want, then? As long as it's in Greek or Latin?
Not quite. There's a bit more to it than that. While the two-part names of a new genus or species can be chosen fairly freely the **full** name of a species can contain twenty or more parts, and describes which higher group, class and family the animal belongs to. In fact, the full name describes a species all the way down to the *kingdom* (animal, plant, fungal, protist or bacterial) that it belongs to.*

A very clever Swedish naturalist called **Carl** (or **Carolus) Linnaeus** first came up with this system back in 1735. He wrote a book called *Systema Naturae* ('natural systems'), in which he began to classify all living things into higher groupings and families, and spent most of his life re-writing and building upon this work. The groupings he used have changed a bit since then (some new ones have been added, while others have been dropped). But

* You can find out more about the Kingdoms of Life in the next chapter.

biologists still use pretty much the same system of classifying and naming living things today – almost 300 years later.

Here's how it works: each **species** is part of a larger **genus**, and each **genus** is part of an even bigger **family**. Got that?

Think so.

Okay. Now each **family** is part of a higher **order**, each **order** part of a **class**, each **class** part of a **phylum**, and each **phylum** part of a **kingdom**.

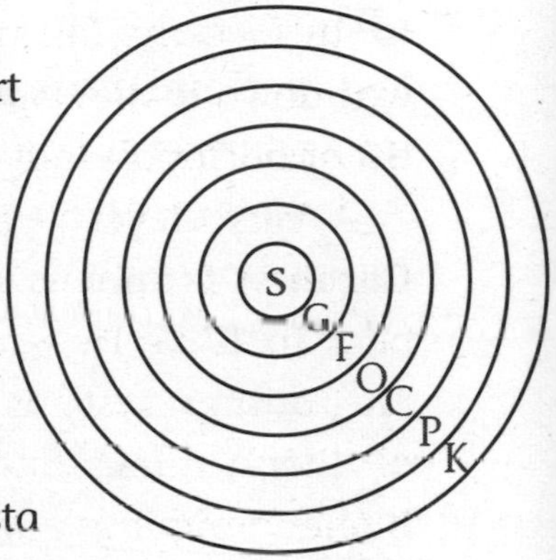

There are six kingdoms of life – Animalia (animals), Plantae (plants), Fungi (er...fungi), Protista (microscopic, single-celled creatures a bit bigger and more complex than bacteria), Bacteria (you know what they are) and Archaea (mega-ancient bacteria that tend to live in extreme places, like volcanoes, salt lakes and glaciers). All – and I mean *all* – forms of life on Earth fall into one of these six kingdoms.

Each **kingdom** has thirty or more **phylums** (or, more properly, **phyla**), and each phylum typically contains several **classes** and **orders**, *hundreds* of **families** and **genuses** (or **genera**) and *thousands* of **species**. Put it all together, and you have *millions* of species (experts guess that there are probably between

5 and 30 million) on the planet. And while we may never get round to naming them all we nonetheless have a system in place for doing it. This system is called **taxonomy**, and these naming groups are called **taxonomic groups**.

So you can name *anything* like that? Anything at all?

Yep. Here are a few examples for you, so you can see how your pet cat (or domestic cat) compares with an African lion, and a common chimpanzee with a human being.

TAXONOMIC GROUP				
Kingdom	Animalia	Animalia	Animalia	Animalia
Phylum	Chordata	Chordata	Chordata	Chordata
Class	Mammalia	Mammalia	Mammalia	Mammalia
Order	Carnivora	Carnivora	Primates	Primates
Family	Felidae	Felidae	Hominidae	Hominidae
Genus	*Felis*	*Panthera*	*Pan*	*Homo*
Species	*catus*	*leo*	*troglodytes*	*sapiens*
Common name	cat	lion	chimp	human

Wait a minute – most of those groups are the same, aren't they?

That's right, they are. And that just shows you how closely related these animals are.

To sum up:

- All four are **Animalia** (animals), **Chordata** (things with backbones or spinal cords) and **Mammalia** (hairy things which make milk, otherwise known as mammals).

- Then you get a two-way split, as the cat and lion are both **Carnivora** (meat-eaters) and **Felidae** (cats), while the chimp and human are both **Primates** (large-brained tree-climbers with thumbs) and **Hominidae** (large, tailless apes which use their hands for gathering food, and sometimes use tools).

- Only when you get down to the level of the genus do you see them split into four totally separate groups – *Felis* (small cats), *Panthera* (big cats or panthers), *Pan* (chimpanzees) and *Homo* (humans or human-like apes).

How different would two animals have to be before they're in different classes, then?

To see a difference in **class**, you'd have to compare one of these mammals with a crocodile (class **Reptilia**),

bird (class **Aves**) or newt (class **Amphibia**). For a different **phylum**, you'd need something without a backbone or spinal cord, like a wasp (phylum **Arthropoda**) or jellyfish (phylum **Cnidaria**). And for a different **kingdom**, you'd need a plant, fungus, protist or bacterium.

Whoa. This is all a bit much. How are you supposed to remember all this stuff?

The good news is that you don't have to. Knowing some of these groupings can be handy for recognizing animals and other living things. And this, in turn, can help you see how one group might have evolved into another. But knowing *every* name is not that important, unless you want to be a zoologist or taxonomist.

But if you want to learn a bit about animal life – and impress your friends next time you go to the zoo the best way is to give it a go (see below). Once you've done that, we can continue our quest to explore the entire animal kingdom.

You mean the kingdom Animalia, right?

Right you are. See – you're getting it already!

DIY zoology

Have a go at classifying the animals below, by putting them in the groups that fit all their features.

- diagram with overlapping, labelled circles
- largest circle is kingdom Animalia
- within this, phylum Chordata (things with back-bones) and Arthropoda (things with jointed legs)
- within these, class Mammalia, Reptilia and Amphibia; on other side, Insecta and Crustacea
- within Mammalia, orders Carnivora, Primates, Rodenta
- within these, families Ursidae, Felidae, Hominidae, Pan

Examples:
1 Snow leopard (*Uncia uncia*)
2 Human (*Homo sapiens*)
3 Common chimpanzee (*Pan troglodytes*),
4 New England lobster (*Homarus americanus*)
5 Polar bear (*Ursus maritimus*)
6 Red-tailed bumblebee (*Bombus ternarius*)
7 Black rat (*Rattus rattus*)
8 *Tyrannosaurus rex*

Why are animals all different shapes and sizes?

Because they've been mutating and evolving for millions of years – slowly adapting to fit every possible environment, diet and way of life. All the different animal shapes have come about through changes in genes and DNA – some big, some small – plus a whole lot of natural selection.

Mutating animals? You're telling me there are mutant animals all over the planet?
Yes. Absolutely.

Yaaaaaaaaaaaagh! Run for your life!
Whoa, there – easy, tiger! What's all the panic about?

Are you crazy? Mutant animals! I've seen 'em in the movies and in video games. They're all twisted and mangled, and they eat people, and . . .
Hang on – not those kinds of mutants.* I just meant animals that had mutated – or changed – from one

* Actually, outside of movies and video games, these kinds of mutants don't really even exist – so I wouldn't worry about them too much, either.

generation to the next, through natural processes.

Oh. So . . . not . . . mutated by mad scientists with chemicals and radiation and stuff?
Er . . . no. Just natural changes in their genes (or DNA) that happen all the time, all by themselves.

Phew. That's a relief. Okay – on you go, then.
Thank you. Now where was I?

As I was saying, evolution is really all about mutating genes. This is something even Darwin didn't know. But genes are at the root of all natural selection, and they're the reason why animals (and all other living things) end up looking different from each other.

Darwin *didn't know* that? I thought he had evolution sussed?
Not all of it. Darwin knew that animals naturally changed from one generation to another. And he also knew that they pass these changes (or mutations) to their offspring. But he didn't know how or why they mutated, nor how the changes were passed on.*

---

* In fact, this has happened fairly recently. After factories were built in northern England in the late 1880s, the majority of the local peppered moth population shifted from speckly brown-and-white to almost black. It turned out that the darker ones were camouflaged better on the newly soot-blackened tree trunks. Now, with less pollution from factories, the populations are shifting back to their original, lighter colour.

Not being able to explain this made it difficult for him to defend his theory of relationships and evolution between animal groups. It's easy, perhaps, to imagine the gradual change of a moth's wings from brown to black . . . And it's almost as easy to imagine a moth mutating into a butterfly, a bee into a wasp, even a wolf into a dog. But the jump between lobsters and llamas, jellyfish and elephants, prawns and people . . . that takes some getting your head around.

Hmmm . . . I see what you mean. So how *do* you get from a prawn to a person? I mean, they're totally different, aren't they?

The answer lies in their DNA, in their genes.

All living things contain DNA – it's in every living cell in everybody (and everybody's body!). DNA is arranged into genes – instructions that tell each growing cell (and ultimately the whole animal) how to build itself. Now the DNA in a cell copies itself every time a cell divides. But

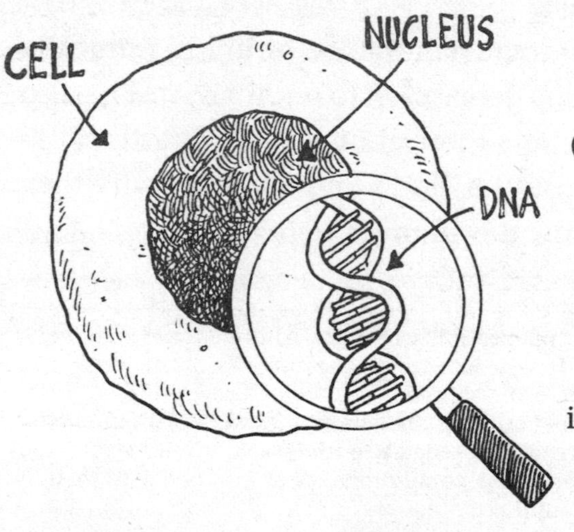

it doesn't do it perfectly. It makes mistakes, which causes changes (or mutations) in the genes. When this happens, a number of cells may receive the wrong building instructions, causing changes (or mutations) in the animal's body.

Like an extra arm or leg?

Usually, it's not as drastic as that. Sometimes mutations do nothing, sometimes they cause big changes. It depends on the gene, and the type of mutation.

Now, one set of genes in particular – called master control genes – pretty much spell out the instructions for an animal's entire body plan. They tell the growing embryo where to put the head and tail end, how many arms, legs or wings it should have (and where they should go), how the guts, bones and nerves develop . . . the works. If these genes mutate, the animal's body plan can be changed enormously.

For example, one set of genes decides which side of the body the spine and the guts will end up on. In humans and other vertebrates, the backbone – of course – goes at the back, while the guts run down the ventral (or belly) side of the body. But in prawns, lobsters, spiders and other **arthropods**, it's the other way around. These animals don't have backbones, of course. But they do have primitive spinal cords (or notochords) that run through their bellies, while their guts run along their backs. If you've ever eaten prawns, you may have noticed this. Sometimes, you find a little 'vein' running down their backs, right? Well, that's actually their gut (which is why it's best to cut this out before eating them – who wants to eat prawn poo?), sitting where the spine would be in a reptile or mammal.

So how did that happen?
This happened because at some point in the past the animal that eventually evolved into prawn had its body plan flipped upside down, because – and this is the important bit – two of its master genes were mutated. So all at once you've had a fork in the road. One led to a group of animals (fish, amphibians, reptiles, birds and mammals) with backbones in their backs and guts in their bellies, while the other led to animals (prawns, lobsters, spiders and other arthropods) with guts in their backs instead.

So in a way people are like upside-down prawns?
Exactly! And it's changes like this that have led to the huge variety of animal body plans that you see around you today. Everything from a bell-shaped jellyfish to a tubular eel. From a four-legged hippo to a two-legged human.

Wow. Giant tube-fish and two-legged, mutant prawn-people. They should make a video game out of that. Or a movie at the very least . . .

If a polar bear and a grizzly bear had cubs, what colour would they be?

This does sometimes happen, and the cubs usually have white bodies and brownish legs. Animals of different species can occasionally mix and mate this way, and sometimes – just sometimes – this can result in the creation of a new species. But, unfortunately, with some exceptions, the genes from different species generally don't mix too well, which leaves them unable to have healthy offspring.

Awww – that's a shame. I thought they might look a bit like big, fuzzy, brown-and-white pandas or something. We could call them polar grizzlies. Or polar pandas . . .

Nope. I'm afraid not. Probably a good thing too, as polar pandas wouldn't be too well camouflaged on the Arctic ice. Even then, the real 'polar grizzlies' are very rare, and most – if not all – are sterile, so they can't form a whole new species. And this, it turns out, is quite common when you mix two separate species.

Why doesn't mixing species work, then?
Firstly, each species usually prefers only to mate with its own kind. Secondly, even when they do mate, it rarely turns out well.

This is because if two groups of animals are separated long enough to form two separate species, that means at least some of their genes have mutated in separate directions. When this happens, the two species' genes become more and more different from each other. So when they're brought back together – on the rare occasion that two different species decide to mate – they no longer match up. Or, at least, the genes no longer work together to produce a healthy baby animal.

So even if two animals look similar on the outside – like grizzlies and polar bears – they still can't have cubs, because they're still too different on the inside? In the genes?
Exactly! Couldn't have put it better myself. In fact, this is part of the definition of the species in the first place. Basically, a species is a group of similar-looking animals that breed only with each other, but cannot (or will not), breed with other groups – no matter how similar they may appear.

Okay. I get that. It's still a shame, but I get it.

There are exceptions, of course. Like **mules,** which result from crossing donkeys and horses, and **ligers**, which result from mating a male lion with a female tigress.* Mixed-species animals like this are called ***hybrids***. They show that cross-breeding between species (known as ***hybridization***) *is* possible for some animals. But hybrid species are still quite rare, and are usually infertile, so they can't have young of their own, and so cannot lead to whole new species.

Male mules, for example, are infertile – which prevents mules from becoming a new species in the wild. And while ligers *are* usually fertile, lions and tigers never interbreed in the wild and so only exist in captivity. Usually in zoos and circuses.

When animal pairings *do* result in fertile young, *sometimes* this can lead to a whole new separate species through hybridization. But as a rule, once two groups have drifted apart into separate species, they tend to stay that way.

But what makes them decide to stop mating with each other? Do they form gangs, or just fall out with each other, or what?

There are several ways groups of breeding animals can become separated. The first is when they're

---

* If you cross a *female* lion and a *male* tiger, you get an even rarer hybrid called a **tigon** instead!

separated *physically*, by rivers, mountains or stretches of sea between islands. We don't usually think of these things springing up quickly enough to affect how things live. But you have to remember that evolution works over thousands or even millions of years – during which time rivers can change direction, sea-levels can rise and fall, and forests can change into deserts. When this happens, the stranded groups of animals can no longer easily reach each other to mate. This has happened many times in evolutionary history, all over the world.

Another way they may separate is when they adapt to different food sources or prey. When different groups start to seek different food sources – even within the same area of land or sea – they can end

up looking very different.* In this case, the animals may live side by side for thousands of years. Until, one day, they have become so different that they no longer look alike, and the females of the species start to prefer animals that look like themselves over their more 'foreign-looking' cousins. And this brings us on to the third way . . .

Sometimes, the females of a species can drive evolution, simply by being choosy. If groups of females begin choosing males with slightly different body shapes or features – and keep doing it for long enough – that alone can be enough to split a species in two. This is especially important in creating new species of birds. (Most of the spectacular bird of paradise species were formed in this way, by choosy females preferring different feather colours and tail shapes.) But this almost certainly happens in *all* animals, *including* humans.

So species split up into new ones because they get *pushed* apart, right? Pushed by rivers, or food sources, or choosy females, or whatever?

That's one way of looking at it, yes. But there's another way it can happen too. They can simply *drift* apart.

By pure chance, even a group in the same region, with the same food (and with non-choosy females),

---

* Just as with Darwin's Galapagos finches, or Wallace's separate (but similar-looking) mammal families.

can split into separate species as their changing genes mutate in different directions. There's nothing obvious happening on the outside, but on the inside it's as if rivers and islands are forming between their genes.

That's a little bit spooky. So could that happen to humans?
In the past, it probably did. But these days – with a few exceptions, like the remote rainforest tribes of Brazil and Borneo – we're all too well mixed together for that to happen. As different as we may look to each other, to natural selection, we're all just one big, happy family.

Ahhh – that's nice.
Yes, it is.

That makes me happy. Not quite as happy as a pet Liger would. But it'll do for now . . .

Spot the hybrid

Some of these animals are real hybrids, made by matings between animals of different species.
Others, I just made up for a laugh.
Can you tell which is which?

Snail	+	Slug	=	Snug
Hawk	+	Squirrel	=	Squawk
Lion	+	Tiger	=	Liger
Jaguar	+	Lion	=	Jaglion
Grouse	+	Owl	=	Growl
Yak	+	Cow	=	Yakow
Scorpion	+	Bumblebee	=	Scumblebee
Zebra	+	Horse	=	Zorse
Donkey	+	Zebra	=	Zeedonk
Bunny	+	Hamster	=	Bumster

(*answers on page 208*)

Which was the first animal to have eyes?

That depends what you mean by 'eyes'. Primitive light-sensing organs or 'eyes' have evolved many times in many different families of animals – and even in a few non-animals. But the first animals with eyes anything like ours were probably a family of fish that are over 450 million years old.

Eyes evolved more than once?
Almost certainly.

There wasn't just one kind of animal with eyes that evolved into all the others?
Well, yes and no.

Mammals, birds, reptiles and other vertebrates have one type of eye, while spiders and insects have a different type, and squid and octopus have yet another. These eyes have very different structures and ways of working, so almost certainly developed separately – probably at different times in evolutionary history. That said, all these types of eyes also share a root in the primitive eye-spots and light-sensitive (or **photosensitive**) patches of more primitive organisms like *protists*.

What do you mean?
Well, some single-celled organisms can detect the

presence of light, but they don't have eyes as we know them. You could say they have a very primitive eye, or 'a bit of an eye' instead, which they nevertheless put to good use.

But what good is a *bit* of an eye? Wouldn't that still leave you blind?

No, it wouldn't. *Partially-sighted*, maybe. But not actually *blind*. There's a big difference.

You see, we tend to think of someone (or something) that can't see shapes or colours – or can barely even make out light and darkness – as effectively blind. But even an animal with the most primitive near-useless eyes can have an advantage over an animal with no eyes at all.

How's that? I mean, they still can't actually *see*, right?

Well, they may not be able to see *much*, but that doesn't mean they can't see anything useful.

For example, there's a single-celled organism called *Euglena*, which has light-sensitive spots within its body. These are simply tiny bundles of proteins that change shape when struck by sunlight. That might not sound like much, but it allows *Euglena* (which gets its energy from photosynthesis, as plants do) to tell whether or not it's in direct sunlight. If it isn't, then it moves around randomly until it is. It 'knows' when it is, of course, because the 'eye spot' proteins change shape.

Hence, *Euglena* can only see one thing – light – yet that's enough to help it survive.

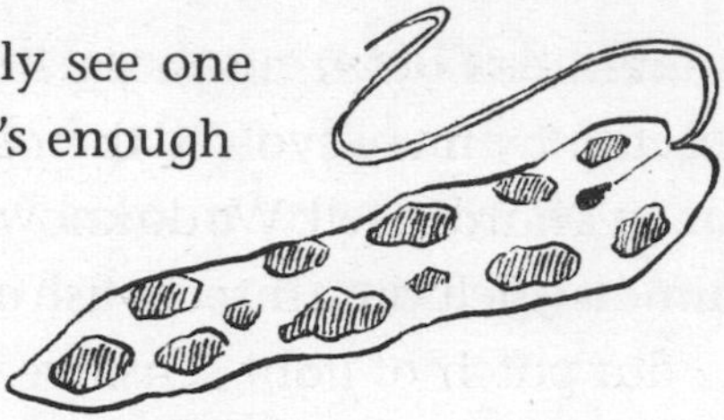

Was that the first animal with eyes, then?

Well, *Euglena* isn't really an animal (it's a protist – different kingdom, remember?). Plus it doesn't really have eyes the way we would define them. **Flatworms** and **sea squirts** (primitive sea animals that live on ocean floors), are another step up from this. They have a patch of photosensitive cells, with which they can tell whether or not a predator is above them, shading out the sunlight. When they sense this, they move away and so may live to wriggle (or squirt) another day.

I guess that would sort of come in handy. So were they the first animals with proper eyes, then?

It's hard to say. As animals go, they're pretty old. But there were a whole load of animals, now extinct, that lived over 500 million years ago that may have had eyes too. Maybe even more complex ones. But since all we have left of them are a few sketchy fossils, it's difficult to tell whether they had eyes at all – let alone how good they were. We know for sure that some ancient fish families, like sharks and rays, had already evolved complex eyes over 450 million years ago. So they may have been the first.

What about other animals, like insects?

Insects may have evolved their eyes before or after the fish – it's hard to tell. We do know that in more complex animals (including insects, fish and other ***vertebrates***), the flat patch of light-sensitive cells has folded in on itself to form a cup or ball. This allows them to make out shadows, shapes and outlines. Spiders and insects combine many of these mini-eyeballs to form **compound eyes**, specialized for detecting movement – which is one reason why it's so difficult to swat a fly. With compound eyes, flies can track our swatting hands almost in slow-motion. So to hit one (little tip for you here) you have to aim at where it's *going* rather than where it *is*. This, incidentally, is more or less what birds do in order to catch them on the wing.

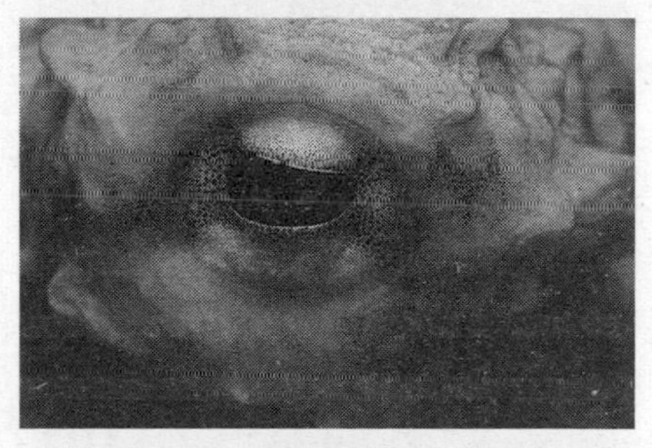

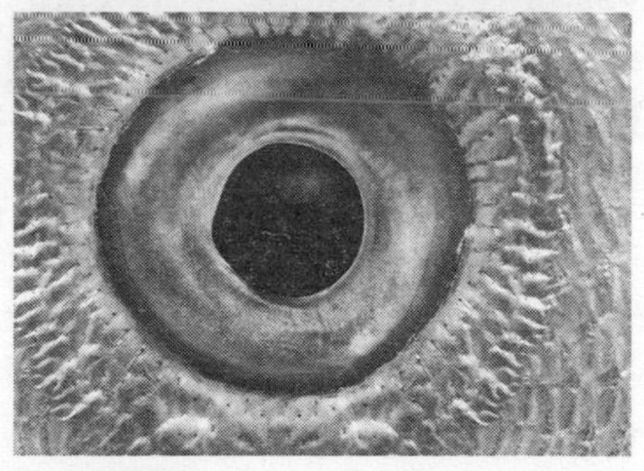

In squid, octopus and other ***cephalopods***,* their cup-like eyes form something like an underwater pin-hole camera. With these, they're able to make out not just shapes, but also fine details and colours – even at huge depths and pressures.

Amphibians, lizards and small mammals are usually colourblind, yet their complex, fluid-filled eyeballs – with lenses for adjustable focus – are advanced enough for most to be able to recognize the shapes and details of specific predators, prey and food sources, even from a distance.

So who has the best eyes of all?

That would be birds and higher mammals – without a doubt. Two forward-facing eyeballs give them 3-D (or *stereoscopic*) vision, allowing them to judge depths and distances. This has allowed them to become faster and more agile, since they can judge

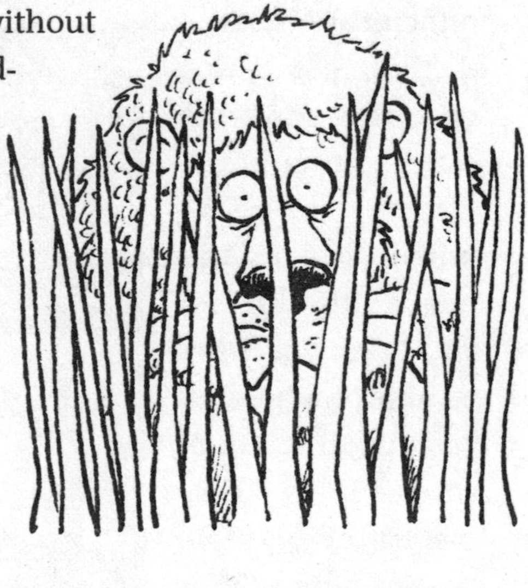

* Cephalopod means 'head-foot' in Greek. They're called this because their feet (or rather tentacles) sprout in a circular bunch from their heads.

their jumps, pounces, dives, dodges and swings better. It also enables them to 'see through' long grasses or trees in forests to track prey hiding within, almost as if they had X-ray vision.

Can't *all* animals do that?
Nope. Believe it or not, most animals can't really do this, and would just see a wall of grass or trees instead. We humans take it for granted, as our eyes (and brains) can focus at different depths automatically.

So our eyes are pretty clever, then?
Yep, they are. Advanced eyes have made birds and higher mammals the most effective hunters on the planet, and may even have *driven* the evolution of our brains, allowing us to move, communicate and even *think* in ways other animals cannot.

Hmm. Eye see. Eye did not know that.
Was that a typo, or are you just being silly?

Eye am not.
Stop that.

Eye-eye, sir!
Arrghhhh!!

Hehehehehe.

Amazing animal eyes

- **Bees** and some other insects can see ultraviolet light, which is invisible to humans and other mammals.
- An adult **peregrine falcon** can spot a tiny rabbit from over 2 miles (3 km) away.
- **Spookfish** have tiny mirrors inside their eyes instead of lenses, which they use to focus images just like reflecting telescopes.
- **Swordfish**, **tuna** and some **sharks** *heat* their eyes when hunting at depth, for extra visual accuracy, with a special behind-the-eye heating organ.
- **Giraffes** have the greatest range of vision of any known mammal.
- While a human eye detects three basic colours (red, green and blue), a cat's eye can only detect two, and most mammals see only in black and white.

If evolution's all about the 'survival of the fittest', then what's the deal with fat, lazy cows and sloths?

Although they don't look too fit, sloths survive because they're very well suited to the environment. Cows, meanwhile, have been artificially selected for survival, for our benefit. When we're talking about evolution, there are lots of ways for an animal to be 'fit'.

I don't get it. How could a cow be well suited for anything? They're so slow and stupid, and people have been herding and eating them for years. Why haven't they evolved into something stronger, faster or cleverer, so they could fight us?

That's because the evolution of cows has been driven not by nature, but by people. The ancestor of all modern cattle, the **auroch**, was a lot leaner and meaner. Now extinct, the wild auroch stood over 2.2 m (6 feet) tall, weighed over 1,000 kg (2,200 pounds) and frequently gored people to death with its

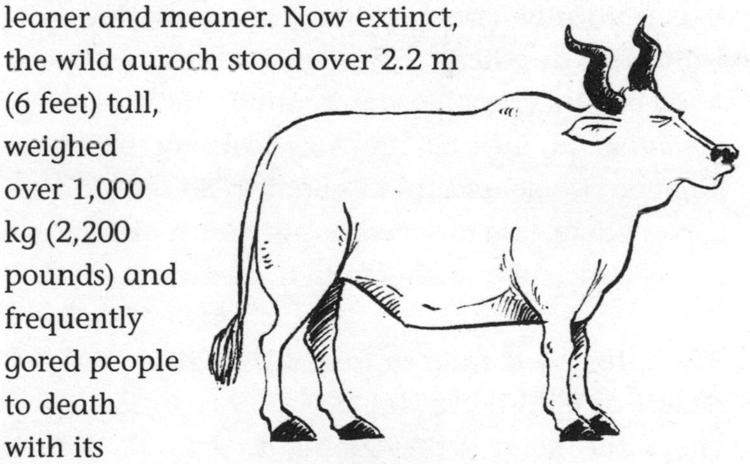

horns. Tackle one of those, and it was just as likely that *you* would end up as minced beef, rather than the other way round.

But over thousands of years, humans chose only the fattest, slowest (and calmest) animals from each generation for breeding. Over time, this has led to a smaller, safer, calmer cow that has now spread worldwide. Meanwhile, the dangerous aggressive cattle – or those too skinny to be useful – have all but disappeared. This is called artificial selection, which differs from *natural* selection because it results in animals best suited to their purpose (i.e. feeding humans). In natural selection, the only purpose the animal has is to survive - so the survivors (rather than harmless, unfit fatties) tend to win out.

What about sloths, then? We don't breed those for food, yet they've evolved to be slow, unfit fatties, like, naturally. They just hang about all day, waiting to be eaten.

Ahh, but they usually don't. Sloths have very few predators in their South American forest homes. Jaguars, people and that's about it. So the predator comes along, and they just hang there looking like a mossy bunch of branches until it goes away.

But if they were fitter or faster, then they could escape or fight back, right?

That's the point – they don't *need* to. A sloth is

well-suited (or fit) for its environment, because its body shape and behaviour allow it to survive very well. Instead of fighting back, it hides and conserves its energy. And in doing so it survives better than many other more active forest mammals.

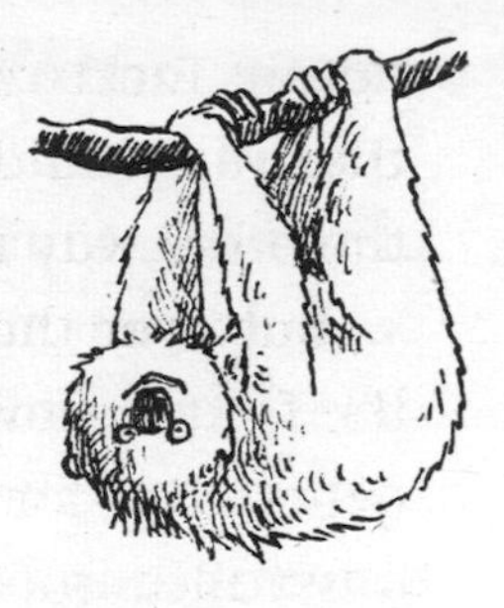

I still don't get it. I mean, in the Olympics, it's the strongest and the fastest that win all the events. So, if survival is like a competition, wouldn't it always be better to be bigger and stronger, anyway?
Not always. Instead of a race or competition, think of it like a war. In a real battle, it's not always the biggest, strongest or fastest soldiers that win the fight. It's often the soldiers with the better weapons, technology and tactics.

But animals don't use weapons, do they? You mean like swinging sticks and throwing rocks and stuff?
Some apes do that, yes. But I'm talking about serious weapons, like blades, body-armour, firepower and chemical weapons.

***What?* Which animals use those?**
Plenty of them. Most cats, dogs, bears and other carnivores have sharp, blade-like canine teeth in their

mouths, and a handful of sharp blades on each paw – as did many large, carnivorous reptiles in the time of the dinosaurs. Mess with those bad boys at your peril. In response, animals like tortoises and armadillos have evolved thick armour plating to protect themselves. The pangolin – a type of tree-dwelling anteater found in Africa and Asia – has even evolved a coat of spectacular, overlapping scales, giving it flexible armour plating that would be the envy of any medieval knight or samurai.

As for firepower, archerfish can shoot dragonflies off twigs with high-pressure streams of water, often with incredible accuracy. Jellyfish and anemones fire poison-filled harpoons into their victims.* Skunks use chemical warfare to deter predators with a foul-smelling urine spray. And many snakes, spiders and other venomous animals can paralyse or kill with their deadly, toothy poisons.

* For more about this, see 'Do sharks eat jellyfish for dessert?' on page 86.

All right, all right, I get the idea. So animals *kind of* use weapons. But come on – none of them have *technology* or *tactics*. I mean, I've never seen a squirrel driving a tank, or an owl flying a stealth fighter . . .

Ah, but they *do* have technology. It might not be *mechanical* technology, but animals have been evolving *biological* technology for millions of years.

Tigers, polar bears and other mammals turn themselves into 'stealth fighters' by blending into their backgrounds with their coat colours. Caterpillars and stick insects imitate twigs and leaves to hide from birds. Chameleons and cuttlefish have adaptive camouflage that can change colour in minutes or even seconds. In fact, the whole idea of military camouflage came from animals in the first place.

The same goes for radar and sonar. Animals (or rather natural selection) came up with these first too. Dolphins and cave swifts use rapid clicking sounds to locate each other and their prey. Bats, famously, can use waves of ultrasound to hunt moths in complete darkness. In response, some moths have joined the arms race by fighting back, using sonar-jamming screams.* Pretty impressive technology for an insect.

As for tactics, you only have to look at a pride of lionesses stalking antelopes, or a wolf pack circling deer in a forest, to see team-tactics in action.

---

* More about this on page 185, in 'Are bats really vampires?'

Dolphins work together to chase fish and chimps manoeuvre small monkeys into traps and ambushes. Many ants, termites and other insects form entire armies, working together to find food or fight off attackers.

In all or any of these ways, an animal can become the 'fittest' in its environment, without necessarily being the biggest, strongest or fastest. As every soldier knows, all it takes to survive is the right gear and the right tactics.

And between them animals have them all, right?
Right.

That explains it.
Explains what?

My mum said yesterday that my goldfish needs a new tank. Maybe they're getting ready for an attack. I'm not sure they'll know how to drive it, though . . .
Groan!

Heheheheh.

Fit for battle

Match each animal with its own secret weapon for survival

hyena	body armour
ibex	teeth
warthog	camouflage
tiger	antlers
bat	deadly venom
cobra	tusks
skunk	ultrasound
pangolin	chemical spray
leaf mantis	claws

(answers on page 208)

4.
The Kingdoms of Life

If all living things are related, does that mean my great-great-grandad was a worm?

Not quite. The great 'tree of life' does connect every living thing in the world – all the way down to fish, worms, sponges and bacteria. But different families of animal lie on different branches of the tree. So while we share ancestors and relatives with chimps, mice – even worms and jellyfish – we didn't evolve directly from the ones you see around you today.

Hold on – so all animals, including humans, *are* related?
Right.

. . . and before we were human, we were more like chimps, right?
Right. And before that, we were more like lemurs. And before *that*, more like shrews.

Okay, so my great-great-grandad was a shrew, then.
Well, I'm pretty sure your great-great-grandad was human . . .

Oh, you know what I mean. Further back than him. Like, my great-great-great-great-great . . .

Okay, okay, I get it. Go back far enough, and you will find non-human ancestors in your family tree. In fact, you only have to go back 5,000 generations (or about 100,000 years) before you reach our most recent non-human ancestors – the human-like (or **hominid**) ape-men known as *Homo erectus*. But you have to go back another 6 or 7 million years before you come across the ancestor we share with modern chimpanzees. (To name that ancestor, you'd have to add 300,000 'greats' to your 'grandad', and it would take you around an hour and a half to say it in full!)

To reach your most recent shrew-like ancestor, you'd have to go back 140 million years, or over 7 million human generations – the time of the early dinosaurs. You'd have to add so many 'great-greats' to *that* grandad that it would take you almost three months, speaking non-stop, to say *his* name.

But here's the thing, neither your chimp-like ancestor nor your mouse-like ancestor were actually chimps or shrews. At least not as we recognize those species today. Just as we have evolved over the millions of years since the time of those ancestors, so have modern chimps and mice. So, while it's correct to say that we have *chimp-like* or *rodent-like* ancestors, it's not true – as many people believe –that our ancestors were chimps and shrews.

Hmm. Not sure I get that.
It can all get a bit confusing. But understanding the difference between the trunks, branches and twigs on the great 'tree of life' can help you to sort it all out. And that's where all that grouping and classification stuff comes in really handy.

Grouping animals together into families, classes and (ultimately) kingdoms allows us to talk about whole groups or related animals at once. So while we *can't* say your great-great-(insert 140-million more 'greats' here)-grandfather was a mouse . . . we *can* say that he was a rodent-like mammal, similar in appearance to a modern mouse.

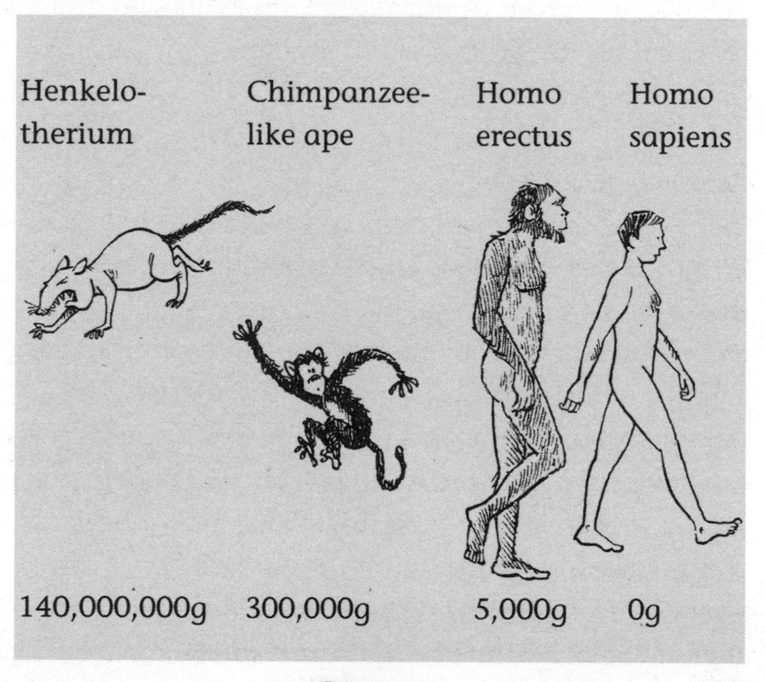

In fact, this rodent-like ancestor – known as *Henkelotherium* – looked more like a tiny (7 cm-long) weasel, and had more in common with **marsupial mice and rats** found today in Australia and New Guinea. It may even have kept its young in a pouch, like a kangaroo!

So my ancestor was really a micro-weasel? Cool! So what came before that?

Another 140 million years before the time of *Henkelotherium*, we have animal ancestors that were reptiles. And over 100 million years earlier than those, amphibians and bony fish.

And before *that*?

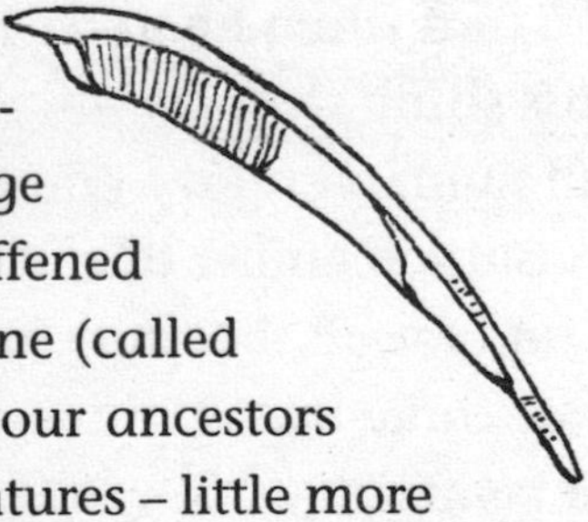

Before fish, there were ancestors that looked like modern tunicates, also known as 'sea squirts'. These are fleshy, tubular animals that spend most of their lives stuck to a sea bed. But during their young larval stage they swim like sea worms stiffened with a primitive type of spine (called a **notochord**). Before that, our ancestors were aquatic, wormlike creatures – little more than a head, bum and gut-tube surrounded by squishy muscle. And before that: sponge-like blobs, living mats of yeast-like goo and lonely, single-celled bacteria.

So my great-great-grandad wasn't really a worm, but I do have worm-like things in my family tree?
Exactly.

And the further back in time you go, the hairier, fishier and slimier our ancestors get, right?
Er . . . I suppose you could say that, yes.

That makes sense.
Why do you say that?

Well, my grandad has hairy ears . . .
Yes, but that's not because—

. . . and sometimes his breath smells of fish . . .
Hang on, that's not very—

. . . and when he takes his false teeth out there's this slimy stuff . . .
All right, all right – enough! I get the picture.

But remember this: if it wasn't for your granddad – and for all the hairy, fishy, slimy animal ancestors that came before him – you wouldn't be here at all. So be nice.

If one species owned the planet, which one would it be?

That depends on what you mean by 'own'. Perhaps most people would argue humans own the Earth, since we've altered and tamed our home planet so successfully. But by almost any other measure we'd be losers to insects, microscopic worms and bacteria.

Wait a minute – that can't be right. Bugs and bacteria? That's not what I meant.
Then what did you mean?

All right – look at it this way. Dinosaurs ruled the Earth for millions of years, right?
Well, in a way, yes. Dinosaurs and other large reptiles were – right up until 65 million years ago – very successful species. Among large animals, they reigned over the land, air and sea for over 250 million years. But . . .

Exactly. They *owned* the place. And then they all died . . .
Well, not *all* of them died . . .

Yeah, yeah – whatever. The point is, they didn't own the Earth any more, did they? So what took over after they were gone?
Well, once the larger dinosaur species had started to

die out, the mammals – who had been living side by side with dinosaurs for thousands of years – finally had a chance to thrive. They started out small, but soon got bigger and spread out to fill the gaps left behind by the giant reptiles . . .

I knew it! So now mammals own the planet! First it was mammoths and sabre-toothed cats, then it was elephants and lions and bears and wolves . . .
Hold on –

. . . then *we* came along and learned to hunt them. And we built farms and cities and space shuttles and . . .
Hang on, hang on – we're getting a bit ahead of ourselves, here. We humans have done a lot in our short time on the planet. But that doesn't mean we own the place.

Why not?
Well, let me put it this way. Let's imagine that the Earth was the set for a huge reality TV show . . .

Started by aliens or something?
Yes – if you want. So all the world's living species are contestants, and after a few billion years the aliens return to pick the winners. In the final judging, it's highly unlikely they'd pick the human species. Or even a mammal.

That's because, for all our accomplishments, we're still just *one* species, with around 6.5 billion members. Which sounds very impressive, until you realize that even among animals, arthropods (insects, spiders, crabs, lobsters and others) outnumber us by trillions to one. In fact, over 90% of all animal species are arthropods. And since these species reproduce so much faster than mammals do, their combined numbers far outweigh us puny, slow-breeding mammals. Expert entomologists (biologists who study insects) reckon there are over **100,000 trillion ants** in the world – so *ants alone* outnumber us by over 20 million to one!

And that's not all. If you go beyond the animal kingdom, then plants outnumber animals many times over. Imagine counting up every tree, bush, flower and blade of grass on land. Now add the many thousands of other aquatic plant species lurking unseen beneath the ocean. As you may have guessed, the numbers get very big, very quickly. And even

without counting we know the volume of plants in the world far outweighs that of large, meat-eating mammals like humans and sabre-toothed tigers.*

How can we know that?

Thanks to a biological rule of thumb about food chains. The general rule is that in each step up the food chain, 90% of the energy is lost. Therefore, it takes ten times the weight of herbivores (or plant-eaters) to support the equivalent weight of one carnivore (or meat-eater). Hence, you need ten times the weight of a lion (in antelopes), or ten times the weight of a shark (in small fish) for the carnivores to survive.

So . . .

So now those herbivores all need to eat too. But since 90% of the energy they get from eating (land or marine-based) plants is also lost, then you need at least ten times as many plants (by weight) as you have herbivores. This also means that each carnivore needs at least 100 times its own weight in plants growing at the bottom of the food chain. And if you add more carnivores in the middle – like the famous picture of a little fish being swallowed by a chain of ever-larger fish swimming behind – then you have more steps

---

* Of course, being extinct, the total weight of sabre-toothed cats in the world is zero. Unless you count the bony remains propped up in museums around the world. And, sadly, that still wouldn't amount to very much.

in the chain. So as each step down requires ten times as much energy and material, one large carnivore (like a Kodiak bear or great white shark) may require over 1,000 times its own weight in plants to support itself. Hence, there are almost certainly hundreds or thousands more plants than there are animals in the world.

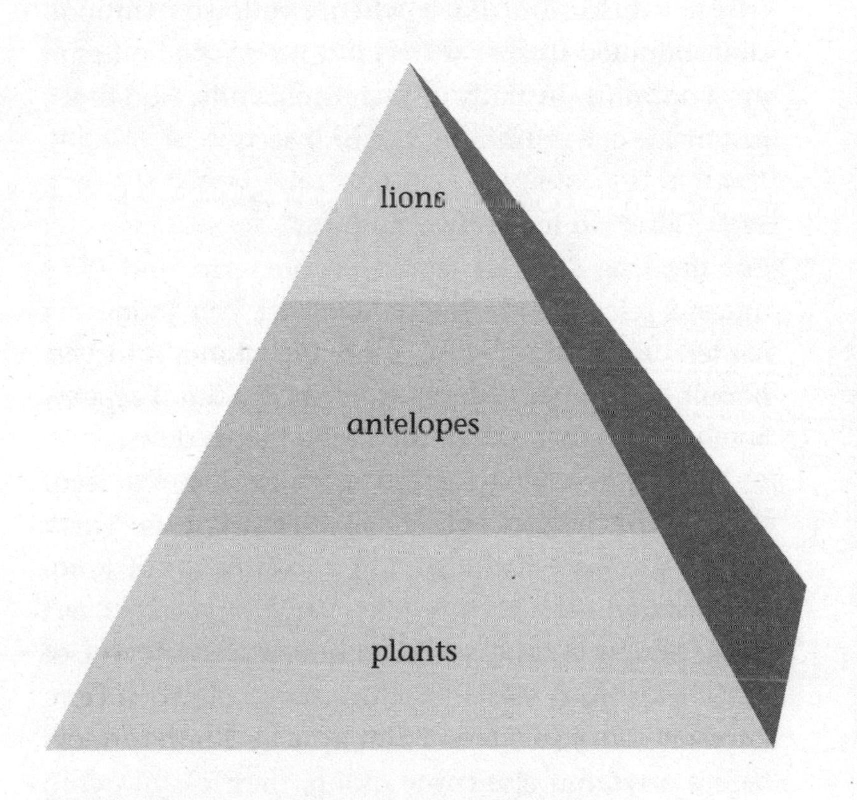

So then . . . *plants* rule the world?

Maybe. They certainly have a stronger claim on it than mammals. But to find the real winning species,

we have to go microscopic. Some microscopic animals, like some **nematode worms**, may be even more numerous than plants if you count them all individually.* **Protists** – single-celled organisms much like larger, more mobile bacteria – are even more numerous still. Disease-causing protists like *Plasmodium* (which causes malaria) and *Giardia* (which causes diarrhoea when swallowed through contaminated food or water) live *within* the bodies of most animals – usually in their thousands. And that's just inside *one* mammal, bird or insect!

Wow. That's a lot of tummy bugs.

But the true winners would be **bacteria** and their ancient relatives, **archaea**. Whether you judge the contest using 'most species on the planet', 'largest population on the planet' or even 'finders keepers', bacteria and archaea would win it hands down.

These hardy, single-celled organisms might seem simple, but they live practically *everywhere* on Earth – places animals couldn't hope to survive for long. Not just in deserts, forests, lakes and deep oceans, but inside rocks, boiling volcanic geysers and layers of glacial ice. And, most importantly of all, they were here first. They ruled the Earth for over 2 billion years before anything else came along, they're still going

---

* For more on these, see 'How do worms breathe underground?' on page 92

strong today and they will almost certainly be here long after we (and most other species) are gone. If the Earth is finder's keeper's, then keep it they will.

I can't believe it. All of us. *Owned*. By *bugs*. Pah.
Look on the bright side. At least they're not smart enough to charge us rent.

Try this:

A complete history of life, using your own body.

- Spread your arms apart as wide as you can, your hands and fingertips extended.
- Now imagine that the span of your arms represents a timeline – the complete history of the planet Earth. This starts, 4.6 billion years ago, at the tip of the middle finger on your left hand. From there, it runs left to right along the length of your left arm, across your body and across your right arm to end at your right middle fingertip, at the present day.
- From your left middle fingertip to your left elbow is about a billion years. For that time, there was nothing but rocks and chemicals on Earth.
- From your left elbow (3.6 billion years ago), right across to your right elbow (about a billion years ago), there was nothing but single-celled bacteria and protists. For that whole time, they ruled the Earth alone.
- Between your right elbow to the base of your

right palm, multicellular life forms (like sponges) began to appear.

- Between the base of your palm (600 million years ago) to the base of your fingers (200 million years ago), primitive marine organisms like jellyfish and corals evolved into complex arthropods, fish, amphibians and reptiles – including, eventually, the dinosaurs.
- The dinosaurs reigned the Earth for the entire period from the base to the last knuckle of your middle finger (around 50 million years ago). From there to the tip of your fingernail, mammals evolved from tiny weasel-like creatures into higher mammals, including great apes and early humans.
- The entire history of the human race – from our caveman ancestors, through ancient Greece and Rome, the Dark Ages, the Middle Ages, the European colonization of America and the New World, the Napoleonic Wars, the two World Wars, the Space Age, the Internet Age and the new millennium . . .

. . . *all* of it could be removed with the *single stroke* of a file, across the tip of your right fingernail.

Kind of makes you think, doesn't it?

Simple, single-celled bacteria ruled the living world for almost all of its history. And we humans have hardly been here for any time at all . . .

Why are trees and plants all green, but mushrooms are white, brown or red?

Because mushrooms are not plants. Nor are they even especially related to plants. They sit in their own kingdom of life – fungi – and are actually closer cousins to us animals!

***What?* Oh, come off it. You don't expect me to believe that.**

Believe what?

That mushrooms are animals. I mean, when was the last time a mushroom ate anyone? Do they creep around the forest stalking mice and rabbits while we're not looking? Don't be daft. This is a wind-up.

It's not. Honest! Although they share some features with both, fungi really are more closely related to animals than they are plants. It's true that – like trees and flowers – they tend to stay put throughout their lifetimes. But it's what they *do* while they sit there that makes them so different to plants . . . and more similar to primitive animals.

What's that, then?

In short, they're scoffers, not growers. Consumers, rather than producers. They get their food and

energy in a very different way.

Plants basically feed themselves. They use a green-coloured chemical called **chlorophyll** to trap energy from sunlight. Then they use that energy to convert water and carbon dioxide gas, from the soil and air around them, into sugars and oxygen. Then they eat the sugars and release the oxygen. Which is very nice of them, because without this process – known as **photosynthesis** (or 'light-building'), we wouldn't have any oxygen to breathe. Billions of years before we came along, photosynthesis by plants, bacteria and protists turned the Earth's atmosphere from a murky veil of noxious carbon dioxide into oxygen-rich air fit for animals to breathe. Plants and bacteria that can photosynthesize and self-feed like this have a special biological name – *autotrophs* (meaning 'self-feeders'). So we owe the autotrophs. Big time.

So how are mushrooms any different?

Mushrooms, toadstools and other types of fungi don't photosynthesize. At all. Like animals, they're *heterotrophs* (or 'other-eaters'). They eat the sugars thoughtfully provided by plants and other self-feeding things.

But why can't they just feed themselves, like plants?

They didn't evolve to. Unlike plants, they can't photosynthesize – because they lack the green chlorophyll

chemical they'd need to do it. (This is also, incidentally, why fungi are usually not green, as almost all plants are.) So, instead, fungi feed on plant and animal wastes, or upon their dead, decomposing bodies.

They eat rotten, dead bodies and poo? Ugh!

Very often, yes. (Bet you won't look at the mushrooms on your fry-up quite the same way again, eh?) But most often mushrooms feed on leaf litter around tree roots, or attach themselves to still-living trees and plants themselves in order to feed on its waste products.

Doesn't that hurt the tree?

Sometimes, yes. Some fungi are parasites which damage or kill the plants they grow on. For this reason, farmers and gardeners spend billions of pounds every year on anti-fungal sprays and soil additives. But others form a kind of friendly partnership, called a *symbiosis*. Some fungi attach themselves to plant roots and extend finger-like threads into the surrounding soil to absorb water and nutrients. The fungus then passes these to the growing plant, which returns the favour by supplying it with sugary food and minerals.

And if you've ever seen a mouldy-looking red, orange or yellow patch on a bare rock-face, then you've seen another type of symbiosis in action. This is a lichen, and it's a partnership between a fungus and a colony of bacteria or algae. Again, the fungus eats sugars provided by the autotrophic (self-feeding) bacteria, while the bacteria/algae are protected from losing water and drying out by the body of the fungus. In this way, lichens can survive in dry, barren places (like rocky crags and deserts) where plants cannot.

Okay, so fungi *look* like plants, but *behave* more like animals?
Right. Like dolphins and monkeys, plants and fungi share a common ancestor, but they're not the same thing at all. And just as monkeys are more closely related to humans than dolphins, studies of plant and fungal DNA have revealed that fungi are closer to animals than they are to plants.

Which, to me, comes as no surprise.

Why's that?
I've always thought of myself as a pretty fun guy. Fun-guy. Fungi. Geddit?

That was awful.
Sorry. I guess there's not mushroom in this book for gags like that.

Groan.
Heheheheheh.

Is there an animal that multiplies when it's chopped into bits?

Yes! While it is rare, at least two types of animal can do this. The vast majority of animals die if you chop them up. But many reptiles, amphibians, spiders and insects can survive having large bits chopped off their bodies. And among the simpler animal families, some are almost indestructible through choppage!

So if you chop a lizard in two, you get two lizards?

Er . . . no, you definitely don't. Some lizards can survive losing limbs (though they don't enjoy it, so please don't go around testing this). And some think so little of losing their tails that they'll happily allow a predator to rip them off in order to escape being eaten. But you don't get two lizards. Just one very relieved lizard and the dead limb or tail it leaves behind.*

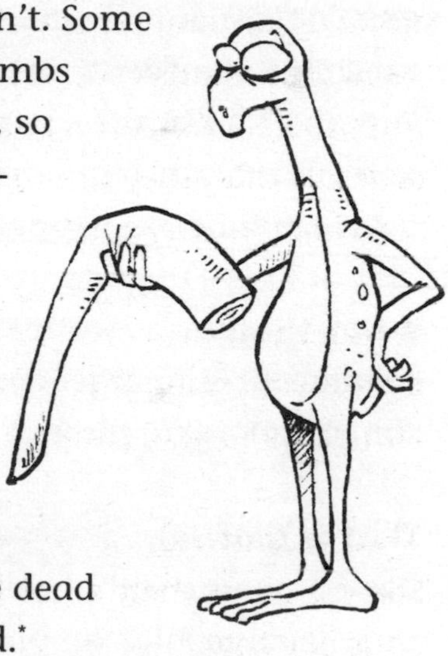

* Happily, most lizard species that do this also *regenerate* their tails again afterwards! Although presumably they don't much enjoy this, since the new tail is usually a bit stumpier, and they can only do this a few times before they end up totally tail-less.

What about snakes?

Despite what you may have heard, snakes will die if you chop them in half, not go on to live in two halves. Depending on where you chop them, some snakes can survive losing a good chunk (up to half the length of) their bodies. But both halves don't live – one (the bit with the head end, with its neural cluster of brain) lives, while the other bit dies.

Does the lost bit grow back?

Sometimes, yes. While snakes cannot generally regenerate (or regrow) lost body lengths, many lizards can and do regenerate limbs and tails from limb buds – in much the same way as animal embryos grow arms, legs and tails in the egg or womb. Some frogs, newts and spiders can regrow body parts too. But none of these animals can survive being chopped into *several* bits, or losing their entire heads. It's not until you get down to starfish, worms and sponges that you see animals able to regenerate their whole bodies from single remaining pieces.

Why is that?

It's all to do with brains. Complex animals like mammals, reptiles, amphibians and insects have large clusters of nerves (or neural tissue) in their heads, which we call brains. Even in the humble lizard or spider, the brain controls essential functions like breathing and blood circulation. Unlike bone and muscle, the brain is very hard to do without, and even harder to replace. Even for very talented reptilian regenerators that regrow lost tissues very quickly, it simply can't be regrown before the rest of the animal's body dies – through lack of blood supply and oxygen.

So how do worms, starfish and sponges do it?

Partly by having even greater powers of regeneration, but also by being less dependent on brains. Worms and starfish don't have brains as such – just small nerve clusters that control bodily functions in much simpler ways. If you cut an arm off a starfish – provided there's still a good chunk of the middle bit (containing the neural cluster) left attached to it – then an entire starfish can sometimes regenerate from that single limb.

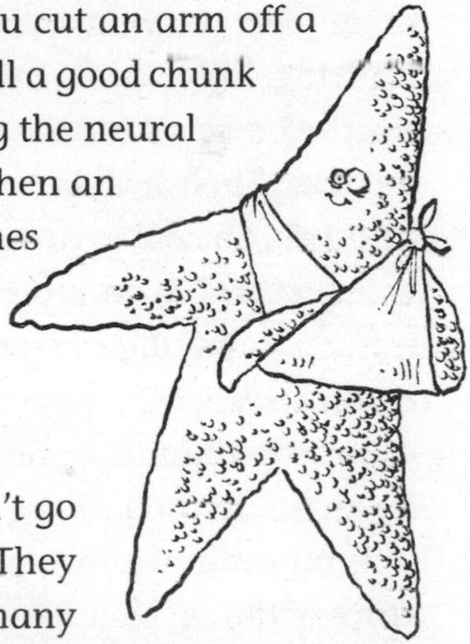

Wow! Cool!

But once again – please don't go to the beach and try this. They really don't enjoy it, and many starfish species will simply die instead. So just take my word for it.

Okay. So how what about worms?

Worms can go one better. Having an even simpler body plan, many types of flatworm can regenerate from any detached body part – head, tail or middle – as long as *some* neural tissue remains. Planaria flat-worms can be sliced in half crosswise or lengthwise, and each half will regenerate into a complete worm. Some can even be cut into several bits, with each one regrowing to form a complete living worm. This would be us losing all four limbs and a head, and re-growing it all from the spinal cord outwards.

Whoa! Freaky!

Sponges, however, probably take the prize. Spong-es are the simplest animals in existence – they're basically little more than clusters of intercommu-nicating cells, formed around a sandy or chalky skeleton. Their bodies can be shapeless blobs, or sim-ple tubes. They absorb nutrients and oxygen from the water around them, and transport it around the body using pumps and channels between the communi-cating cells.

But the animal never moves. It just sits there for life on the sea bed. Until, that is, it reproduces. Then it buds off little swimming sponglets (like little sperm), which swim off to fertilize egg cells released by other sponges, and settles down on a new spot of seabed to grow into a new animal.

But here's the cool thing: you can take a sponge, put it in a blender, shove the bits through a filter and leave them in a tube or tank, and guess what happens! Yep – the sponge will spontaneously reassemble itself like some sort of indestructible alien zombie!

Cool! So could we ever learn to do that?

Unfortunately, humans could never survive the 'blender treatment', since our bodies are way too specialized. Even worms are too complex for that one. But scientists are studying starfish, salamanders and other regenerating animals in an effort to find out how they regrow muscle, bone and nerve tissue. It's hoped that one day, we might figure out exactly how they do it, and create drugs to trigger ancient genes, lying deep within our DNA, that cause damaged limbs, organs and brains to repair themselves through regeneration.

That would be brilliant!

Indeed. But until they do figure it out I'd avoid doing anything that might result in lost limbs. Like playing with samurai swords. Or jumping into blenders.

Do sharks eat jellyfish for dessert?

No, they don't. While some turtles eat jellyfish, sharks and other fish tend to avoid them, as eating one feels much like munching down a slimy stinging-nettle salad.

Ouch. That doesn't sound too tasty. Not a bit like jelly and ice cream.

Not at all. Unfortunately for sharks, jellyfish don't come in lime and strawberry flavours. Come to think of it, even if they did, it's still not clear whether sharks would dig them. They'd probably prefer seal flavour, or perhaps surfer's leg flavour.* In any case, jellyfish taste pretty horrible. And, worse still, unless they're carefully dispatched and prepared by a cunning chef,** most jellyfish mount some pretty vicious defences to avoid being eaten.

You mean the stingers?

Right. Or, rather, the stinging cells. Jellyfish belong to a class of animals called *Cnidaria* – the word comes from the Greek for 'nettles'. (See? They really are like living nettle salads!) All Cnidaria carry thousands of specialized stinging cells (or cnidocytes), usually on

---

* This is, of course, just a joke. While they do like seals, sharks don't really like the taste of surfers. They usually just bite them by mistake, thinking they're seals or turtles. See my other book, *Stuff That Scares Your Pants Off*, for more about shark attacks and surfers.

** And even then they still taste horrible. Trust me – I ate one once in Japan. Bleurgh.

the surface of their flailing tentacles. Inside each one is a tiny, microscopic, poison-filled harpoon.

Touching a tentacle (even just barely brushing it) is enough to trigger the weapon. With incredible speed, the harpoon explodes out of the cell like a high-pressure, water-powered rocket. Once inside the target, it wedges itself within the flesh with arrow-like, backwards-facing barbs, and releases its poison into the surrounding tissues and bloodstream. Using these micro-harpoons, a cnidarian can paralyse or kill insects, fish and – occasionally – people. Some turtles, however, have become immune to the stingers. Which is why they – and only they – bother to eat them.

Blimey. That all sounds a bit clever. I didn't think jellyfish were that smart. I thought they were just brainless, drifting blobs in the sea.

Well, in a way they are. Jellyfish and other cnidarians lack anything approaching a real brain. And most are content to drift in ocean currents to find prey and mates – doing little more than controlling their depth with their squidgy, rippling muscle contractions. But for many reasons they're also unique and fascinating animals. A glimpse of our evolutionary past.

How's that, then?

For starters, many cnidarians (not only jellyfish, but also **sea anemones**, **corals** and freshwater **hydras**) are **polymorphs**, or shape-shifters. Their bodies can

take one of two major shapes, and they shift between them at different stages of their lives.

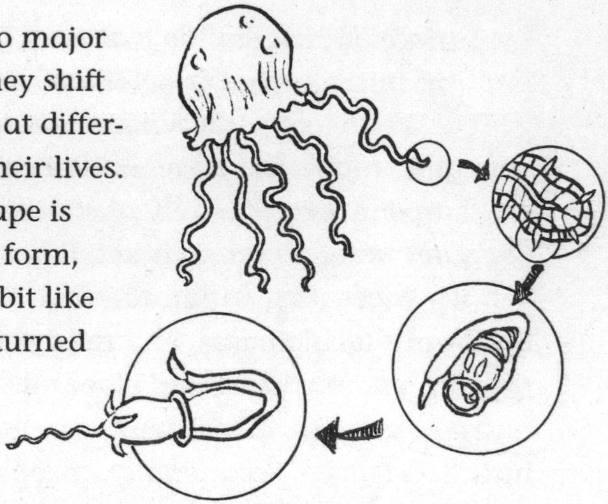

The first shape is called a polyp form, which looks a bit like a flower or upturned sink plunger. Anemones and corals remain in this shape throughout their entire adult lives, stuck upside-down to rocks or seabeds with their stinging tentacles waving in the water. When they reproduce, bits of themselves bud off from the main body and float to another site.

In some species, these baby anenomes and corals stay in the polyp form. But in others they shift to the second shape – the medusa form. This looks much like you'd imagine a jellyfish – like a see-through umbrella without a handle. The medusa form then swims about breeding with others, until it eventually lays a fertilized egg, which in turn becomes another anemone or coral polyp.

Jellyfish, on the other hand, do things the other way round. They spend their entire adult lives in the umbrella shape, then lay eggs which develop into tiny baby polyps. These stay on the seabed until mature, at which point they bud off into a medusa form, which grows into an adult jellyfish.

Okay – this is getting pretty confusing now . . .

It gets better. Cnidarians are among the very few animals with radial (or wheel-like) symmetry. Most animals (humans included) are symmetrical on one side-to-side axis – so you could put a mirror vertically through the centre of our bodies, and we look more or less the same on both sides. Two eyes, two ears, two lungs, two arms, two legs . . . each pair the same basic shape and size. But with jellyfish you could place the mirror vertically through them at *any angle*, and they will look the same on either side of it – like a wheel or a big round birthday cake.

This is also why they lack a single, solid brain. Since they look the same from *all* sides, they could encounter food or predators from *any* side. So there's no point in developing a 'head' end with a brain. Instead, they have rings of nerves that encircle their umbrella-like bodies, forming a **neural net** for basic control over its body systems.

Swimming, poisonous birthday cakes. Weird.

Finally – just to top off the weirdness – jellyfish and anemones also lack guts. So they eat and poo through the same hole.

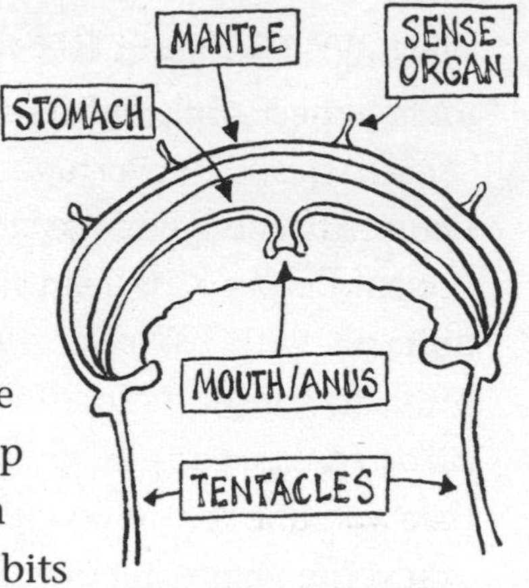

Ugh! Seriously?
Seriously. Anything unlucky enough to drift into their mouths, or into the space beneath their umbrella-like mantles, gets digested and pulled into the tubular oral lobe sticking up (or hanging down) through the centre. Any undigested bits are then spewed (or pooed, depending on how you look at it) back through the same opening.

Gross! So could a jellyfish eat a person?
No. Fortunately, they don't grow big (or hungry) enough to do this. And although a few cnidarians (like fire corals, box jellyfish and sea wasps – see the box opposite) can be harmful to swimmers and divers, most are just a nuisance. Which is fortunate, since jellyfish numbers have been steadily increasing as sea temperatures gradually rise under the influence of global warming. Already, some swimming beaches in Europe and Australia are being closed every year due to annual jellyfish swarms.

No problem – I've got a plan to deal with that.
What's that, then?

Just swim behind a hungry turtle!

KNOW YOUR JELLIES: FACTS ABOUT CNIDARIA

A few species of jellyfish, such as the box jellyfish, the sea wasp and the Portuguese man-of-war, have stings powerful enough to harm humans. Box jelly stings are so painful they can send victims into spontaneous heart attacks.

Clownfish – made famous by the movie *Finding Nemo* – are immune to anemone stings, and make nests among their stinging tentacles to stay safe from bigger fish. Hermit crabs go one better – they often place anenomes on their shells on purpose, creating weaponized, mobile fortresses to ward off fish and octopus attacks!

How do worms breathe underground?

They breathe through their skin. Simple, small animals don't need as much oxygen as larger, more complex ones. So they absorb all the air they need through their outer body surfaces alone. A bit like turning your lungs inside out, and wearing them like a wetsuit.

Ugh! A wearable lung-suit? Gross! I always thought worms were icky. Now I know they are. Is that why they're so slimy, then?

Partly, yes. Worms, you have to remember, first evolved in the sea, where they never had to worry about drying out, and oxygen from the water around them could simply drift (or diffuse) through their bodies. But as they moved out of the water and into the open air, they had to find a way of both staying moist and getting oxygen from the air around them. So they secrete a layer of slimy mucus from their skin, which prevents water from evaporating out, whilst allowing oxygen to dissolve into their bodies.

In this way, worms can not only survive underwater and underground, but also deep inside animal bodies – beneath skin, and inside blood vessels and organs.

Yuck! Like cats and dogs, when they get worms?

Yep, but also inside pretty much every other species of animal on the planet. Including humans.

No way! I don't have worms!

I'm afraid you probably do. If not a big one, like a tapeworm or hookworm, then it's almost certain that some species of microscopic roundworm has set up shop somewhere within your body. Worms, you see, are *everywhere*.

There are lots of types of worms, and they all have their place in the world. **Flatworms** (from the phylum *Platyhelminthes* – literally 'flat worm') are perhaps the simplest. Unlike starfish and jellyfish, flatworms have true guts. They have a head or mouth end, where they take in food, and a tail end where – ahem – wastes are released. They also have a simple nervous system and the beginnings of a spinal cord (which, as we will see in the next chapter, eventually lead to backbones and brains in fish and other, more complex animals). They are also the longest animals in the world – the **bootlace worm** reaches lengths of over 50 m (150 feet)!

Tapeworms lack guts of their own, so instead they use those of other creatures. They live in the guts of fish and farm animals, absorbing partly digested food through their bodies and laying thousands of eggs inside their intestines. When the eggs hatch, the baby worms migrate into the animal's muscles and organs. If we then eat this worm-infested fish or meat, we humans can sometimes harbour tapeworms inside our own guts too – which can stay there for months or years!

Annelids, or segmented worms, are the kind you see squidging their way through soil or dangling from early birds' beaks. Earthworms (see picture) are actually very helpful – eating dead leaves and plant roots, and turning them into fine nutritious soil. They can also grow incredibly long – one species of African earthworm can reach lengths of over 6 m (20 feet)!

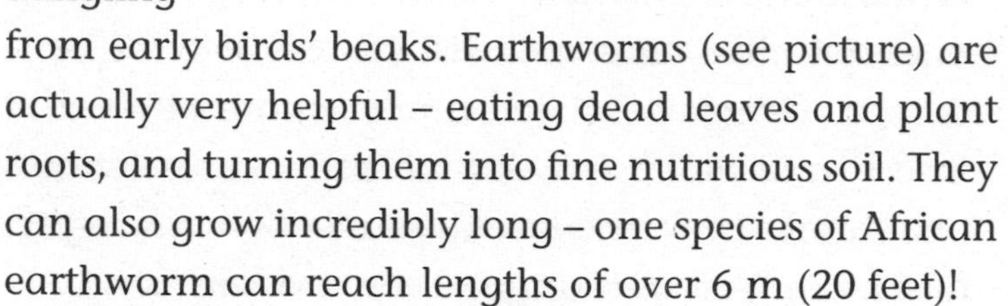

And finally, **nematodes** (or **roundworms**) of various sizes infect humans all over the world. Whipworm eggs are passed from hand to mouth when you don't wash your hands after going to the toilet. (See? Your mum knows what she's talking about.) Pinworm eggs can be inhaled with dust. And hookworms can burrow right through your skin and into your body. Some roundworms are microscopic, while others are over a metre long.

Ewwww! Disgusting!

And that's not all. Roundworms, scientists estimate, are so numerous and widespread that they literally fill the animal world. In fact, if you could magically make all the animal bodies in the world invisible, you could still make out the shape of their bodies, thanks to the number of worms inside them. Like big, wormy sculptures. *That's* how many there are.

Arggh! They're everywhere! It's like a whole world of worms! How did there get to be so many?
Part of the reason for that is that they've been here a very long time – for over 500 million years. Most of the world's complex animals evolved from them. Their primitive guts and head-to-tail body plans led to more complex digestive and circulatory systems in insects and molluscs. And the nerve cords found in one family of worms eventually led to fish, reptiles and mammals with spinal cords and backbones.*

So fish are like worms with eyes and backbones?
In a roundabout way, yes . . .

And reptiles are like fish with arms and legs and lungs?
Well, you could say that . . .

And mammals are like hairy, big-brained reptiles . . . with boobs?
Er . . . sort of, yes.

And most of them still have small wriggly

---

* For more on this, see 'When did fish grow feet?' on page 116.

hitchhikers inside them?
Yes. Something like that.

Ugghhhhh. Well, that's all very interesting – but now I feel all icky. I'm off to take a bath.
Me too. Nothing like a worm to make you squirm.

Build your own wormery

- For a few days, start saving food scraps from the dinner table in a sealed container in the fridge. Keep apple cores, banana skins, orange rinds, potato peelings, leftover carrots and salad leaves . . . any fruit or veg that would otherwise have gone into the bin (but don't add meat – this will make the wormery smell, and may attract rats and other pests).
- Once you've done that, dig up some worms from the garden. Or wait until it rains, then pick them up as they slither to the surface. Put them in a lidded container, along with a little soil. Poke some air holes through the lid.
- Take a clear plastic or glass fishtank, and pour in a layer of dirt until it covers the bottom to a depth of around 5 cm. Now pour in a layer of sand, to roughly the same depth again. Keep it loose – don't pack it in – otherwise your worms won't be able to tunnel (or breathe).

- Put in a layer of your food scraps from the fridge, cover with another layer of soil, another of sand and finally the rest of the food scraps.
- Lob your worms in, put a perforated lid on the tank, and leave them to it. Within a day or two, your worms will start churning the soil, sand and food scraps as they tunnel back and forth. Add more moist food scraps to keep feeding them, or release them into the garden after a couple of months.

Hey presto – a living wormery!

Why are there no car-sized bugs and beetles?

Because of the way their bodies are built. Bugs and beetles are like knights in thick armour. Their heavy outer skeletons are great for protection, but if they're built too big they're too heavy to move.

But insects don't seem very heavy. I mean, you can hardly feel them when they walk on you.
That's because they're usually pretty tiny. But if you think about their larger cousins, crabs and lobsters, you start to get an idea of how heavy a big bug would be.

Crabs, lobsters, spiders, scorpions and insects form part of a larger group of animals called **arthropods**. 'Arthro-pod' literally means 'jointed legs', which describes their knight-in-armour-style body shapes. Arthropods are basically like us, inside out. Instead of having solid bones surrounded by pulling muscles, they have their skeleton on the outside and muscles on the inside. Their exoskeletons are made of a tough protein called chitin, which forms a solid shell around their bodies and hard tubes around their limbs.

But if they're all rigid and stiff, then how do they move at all?

Ahhh, that's where the joints come in. The stiff shells and tubes are jointed, and the muscles that move their bodies are attached to the insides of them. This gives them rigid bodies, but flexible, movable legs. The arthropod's body is built in sections or **segments**, and pairs of limbs stick out from the side or the bottom of certain body segments. The typical insect, like an ant or beetle, has a head, thorax and abdomen, along with three pairs of leg segments, giving them six legs altogether.

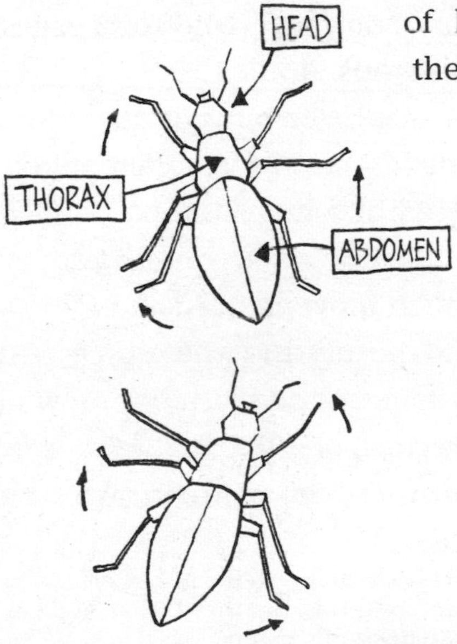

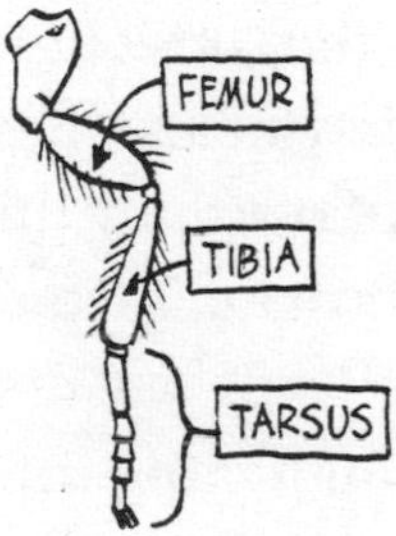

To move, each leg moves (from the 'hip' joint where it contacts the body) up, forward, back, then down in an alternating pattern, driving the insect forward.

For the small insects, this works very well. The hollow, shell-like armour protects them from predators, and they stay mobile. But beyond a certain size, these tubes and shells would buckle under their own weight, leaving them paralysed and vulnerable to attack. That's why insects typically don't get bigger than a few centimetres or inches across. The largest beetles and bugs in the world live in South America and China, and even they rarely reach over 18 cm (7 inches) long. Big enough to be scary, perhaps, but certainly not man-eaters.

But what about spiders, scorpions and millipedes? Some of those get enormous, don't they?

Well, they're not really insects or bugs at all. Spiders and scorpions are *arachnids** and have different body shapes and lifestyles. They also have four pairs of legs rather than three, and use different hunting tactics that don't require so much movement – such as lying in wait on a web and paralysing their prey with stings. Still, the largest spiders and scorpions grow no more than 30 cm (12 inches) across.

Millipedes and centipedes are in their own fam-

---

* This group also includes ticks and mites. To the naked eye, these animals look like tiny dots or beads. But they look a lot more 'spidery' when you put them under a microscope.

ily, the **myriapods** (meaning 'many legs'), and some use their extra legs to support their extra size and weight. African giant millipedes can grow up to 38 cm (15 inches) long. Again, I wouldn't want to find one of these in my bed, but we're still well short of car-sized.

The largest arthropods around are the aquatic ones – the crustaceans. Crabs and lobsters have five pairs of legs (ten altogether), and rely on buoyancy from the water to help support their heavy bodies, so they can grow much larger. North Atlantic lobsters reach up to 60 cm (2 feet), while Japanese spider crabs have bodies over 30 cm across, and a leg span of up to 6 metres (20 feet)!

Now you're talking! That's massive!

Of course not all insects trot along the ground or sea-bed. Some have, very successfully, taken to the air – like flies, beetles, bees, wasps and butterflies. But again there's a limit to how huge they can grow. In fact, as you might expect, getting airborne is even harder than walking or running.

Small insects like bees and wasps fly by beating their wings very rapidly and creating swelling vortices in the air, which help keep them aloft, but then flying is more like swimming through a gloopy liquid than gliding or flapping through thin air. The bigger you get the harder you fall. Or, rather, the harder it is to stay airborne. This is why flying insects no longer get very big at all. The largest wasp in the world* is only 12 cm (5 inches) long, while the largest living flying insect – the Chinese giant water-bug – has a wingspan of around 20 cm (8 inches). Which, admittedly, you'd need a cricket bat to swat. But it's still pretty harmless, and not quite in pterodactyl territory.

What do you mean 'no longer' get very big?
Well, at other times in the Earth's history, some bugs, such as dragonflies, were quite a bit bigger. This was because the atmosphere was warmer and thicker, providing more lift and oxygen for energetic, big-bug flight. Some prehistoric dragonflies reached sizes of up to 70 cm (4 feet) across.

Now *that's* a big bug. So if the world heats up enough – you know, with global warming and stuff – good big bugs like that might evolve again?
It's unlikely, but not impossible. The atmosphere would have to get bigger as well as warmer, and there's no indication that will happen any time soon. That said, supergiant bug-like creatures may exist on some distant planet that we haven't found yet. A planet with a thick enough atmosphere or less surface gravity could support a race of super-sized scorpions or land-crabs – where perhaps they lumber around

---

* Which lives in South America and actually attacks and kills tarantulas. They get all the crazy bugs down there.

picking up people-sized prey in their huge crane-like pincers . . .

Cool! I'd love to see that!

Me too. From a safe distance, mind.

Odd bug out

Spot the odd one out in each group of four animals below.

1. stag beetle	fruit fly	butterfly	millipede
2. daddy long-legs	tarantula	camel spider	deer tick
3. hermit crab	cuttlefish	prawn	lobster
4. dragonfly	spider crab	starfish	barnacle

(*answers on page 208*)

Why are slugs and snails so slimy?

For three main reasons. First, it keeps them from drying out in dry air. Second, it allows them to climb and crawl upside down. And, third, it makes them taste revolting.

But why would they have to worry about drying out?

Because they evolved in water and adapted to live in air. You have to remember that slugs, snails and other **molluscs** first evolved to live in the sea. Most of them – like clams, mussels, limpets, cuttlefish, squid and octopus – simply stayed there. But slugs and snails alone left the water for the air,* and when they did they had to find a way of keeping their bodies moist in the dry air around them.

Part of the solution to this was to secrete a slimy layer of mucus from glands in their skin. This layer then forms a waterproof barrier that prevents water from evaporating out of their bodies.

And also makes them slimy and gross, right?

Right. In fact, some slugs and snails secrete a toxic (or, at the very least, very nasty-tasting) slime that discourages birds, reptiles and mammals from eating

---

* Some mussels can survive in freshwater lakes and rivers, and some molluscs – like limpets – can survive for hours in the open air, between tides, by clamping their shells tightly to rocks. But slugs and snails are the only molluscs that can survive out of the water indefinitely.

them. Although this doesn't seem to dissuade French chefs, who boil off the slime and coat them with butter and garlic instead.

Urrrghhh. I'll never understand that.

Me neither.

So why do snails have shells, but slugs don't?

Because slugs don't really need them.

But why? Doesn't being shell-less leave slugs a bit – you know – defenceless?

Well, for land snails, shells are really more of a protection against drying out than they are against predators. They're too thin to serve as real armour, as they do in clams and mussels. On land, birds and rodents and predators usually just crunch right through the shells, or whack them against rocks until they burst open. It also takes quite a bit of time and energy to make a shell. Not to mention lots of calcium – which means snails can only live in areas with calcium-rich soils and plants.

Slugs, evidently, figured this out. So at some point they stopped making shells, and began secreting a thicker, stickier slime to replace the shell instead. Which – unless you're nasty enough to pour salt on them – protects them from drying out quite nicely.

So slugs used to have shells?
Yes. And, in fact, many of them still do! You just can't see them. Many slug species build thin shell-like layers of calcium *under* their skin (or mantle) – revealing their snail-like evolutionary past.

Besides that, slugs and snails have many other things in common too. They each have a rasping, toothy tongue called a *radula*, some bearing hundreds or thousands of teeth, which they use to snip and scrape at their food.

Snails and slugs have teeth? No way!
Yes, way. How did you think they did that much damage to lettuces and other plant leaves? By sucking on them?

Oh. Didn't think of that . . .
They also have one or two pairs of tentacles (with eyes at the base), plus a single squishy foot that they use for crawling along surfaces. And this is where their slime really comes into its own.

How's that?
The slime works as both an oily lubricant, and a sticky glue. It sticks the slime or snail to almost any surface, allowing it to crawl straight upward, or even upside down, using wave-like rippling motions of its foot.

But if it's glued to the surface, how does it move at all?
As the animal pushes its muscular foot forward, the glue towards the rear of the foot breaks, and the foot peels away. When the animal stops moving, the glue reforms, holding it fast to the surface. So it sort of sticks and slides its way along, leaving a trail of goo in its wake. Lately, engineers have become interested in this unique slime-propelled mode of travel. They've begun studying slug and snail slime with a view to using it for slug-like wall-crawling robots.

Wicked! But . . . er . . . how do they go about collecting snail slime?
Believe it or not, the preferred method is to coax a snail on to a pane of glass with a lettuce leaf, then lead it into making slimy circles, and scoop up the whole trail at the end.

Yuck! I wouldn't want that job. Snails are gross.
You think that's gross? Get this – somewhere along the line of snail evolution, their guts twisted through 180 degrees so that their bums now lie directly above their heads, just beneath the shell. So snails poo on their own heads.

Why would they do that? What are they, stupid or something?
To be honest, no one really knows how or why this

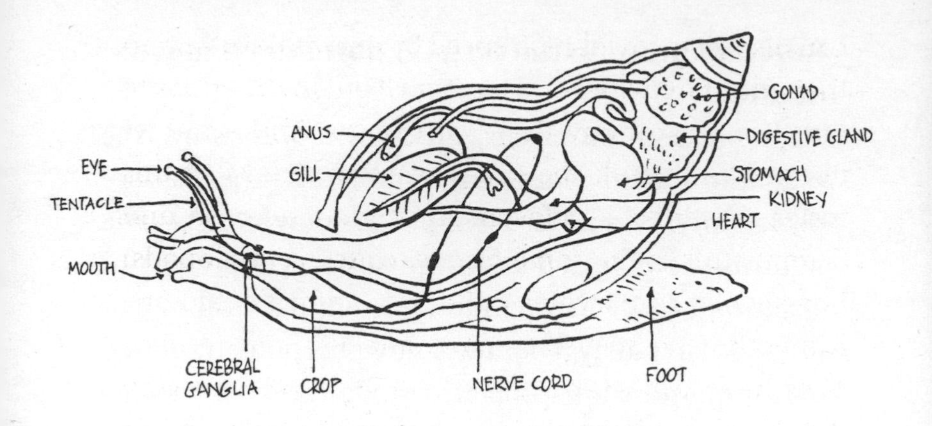

happened. It doesn't seem to make a lot of sense, as it means they constantly risk fouling on their gills – literally breathing in their poo and choking to death on it. But somehow they seem to get by.

So molluscs breathe through gills, then? Not lungs?

Sea snails – and most other molluscs – have gills. But in land snails these have turned into true lungs, which draw air in and out using muscles, much as ours do. Either way, the breathing organs sit just between the head and the shell, on the surface of the **mantle**. In octopus and squid, the largest members of the mollusc family, the pumping gills can also take on another function entirely: jet propulsion.

Really? I thought they just kind of squidged around using tentacles.

Octopuses do crawl on surfaces, but when startled they

can also jet away at high speed by drawing water into their mantle cavities and blasting it out in the opposite direction to the way they want to go. And squid jet about like this all the time. Perhaps thanks to this faster, jet-propelled movement, squid, cuttlefish and octopus (all in the same family, called cephalopods) have evolved to become agile carnivorous predators, rather than passive, slimy plant and plankton feeders. They have keen vision and reflexes, and are also very smart, as invertebrates go. Squid and cuttlefish are known to communicate with each other using light patterns strobed across their bodies, while octopuses have been shown to have a cunning problem-solving intelligence when hunting.

They also get big. Very big. Giant squid grow to over 10 m (30 feet), and regularly do battle with sperm whales. And the recently discovered colossal squid grows to 13 m (40 feet) and perhaps much larger.

Freaky! So if they're so smart and deadly, why have squid and octopus never crawled out of the ocean to live on the land, and – you know – evolved into squid-people or something.

Partly because they couldn't get about too easily. Their water-filled tentacles are adapted to moving underwater, and are floppy and useless on land. (If you've ever seen a squid or octopus out of the water, you'll know what I mean.) Which is probably quite a good thing for we land animals.

What about on another planet? Could it happen there?

Who knows? I do know this – a race of air-breathing squid-people would be scary. Think about it – cephalopods are intelligent, communicative, stealthy and carnivorous. Here, they're kept in check by being unable to leave the water and, even if they did, they'd face large predators and competition on land.

Yeah! Maybe elsewhere they might evolve super-intelligence and superior technology. Then they could mount a full-on alien mollusc invasion! Then what would we do?

Send in the French, maybe. Armed with big dinner forks and blobs of garlic butter.

5.
Big Things with Backbones

Why do crocodiles wriggle when they walk?

Because – like most other reptiles – crocodiles can't rotate their hips or shoulders. So they have to wriggle their spines from side to side in order to 'snake' their way forward. Reptiles are built differently to mammals, so, while they're more agile on land than fish and amphibians, they're a poor second to cats, dogs, horses and humans when it comes to walking, running and jumping.

Why's that? I thought lizards and crocodiles could move pretty fast.

Some can. The spiny-tailed iguana, which lives in Costa Rica, can reach speeds of up to 22 mph (35 km per hour) on land, while freshwater crocodiles can manage up to 11 mph (17 km per hour) at full gallop. But that's nothing compared to mammals. A cheetah can hit a top speed of 55 mph (90 km per hour) over short distances, while gazelles and springboks can maintain speeds of 50 mph (80 km per hour) over

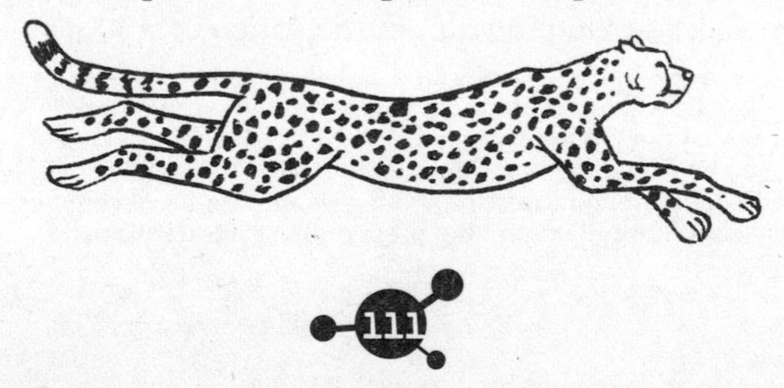

distances of a mile or more. What's more, cheetahs and gazelles can dodge and turn as they do so. No reptile is capable of agility like this.

Why not?

Because of the way their bodies are built and how they have evolved. But rather than just tell you all about it let's do a little experiment . . .

Try this. Lie on the floor, belly down, and let your arms flop loosely at your sides. Imagine you've been bitten by a snake, and your arms and legs are paralysed. You can't feel them or move them at all. Now try moving your whole body across the floor, just using your shoulders, hips, and the wriggling of your spine. Go on, try it. I'll wait.

(Hmph! Grunt! Wheeze!) Whew! That's hard!

Not too easy, is it? But this is pretty much all a fish can do (and explains why fish don't move too well on land!). Fish are the simplest vertebrates (or things with backbones). They can wriggle their spines, but that's about it. In the water, that allows them to swim and turn, but on land spine-wriggling alone isn't much cop.*

* Some fish, like **mudskippers**, can flip about on the shore reasonably well at low tide, jumping distances of up to 60 cm (2 feet) by wriggling their spines and pectoral fins. But even they aren't agile enough to escape two-legged human beachcombers, who casually stroll up and flip them into buckets for dinner.

Now let's try evolving into a reptile . . .

Get on the floor once again, this time on all fours, with your hands and feet touching the ground. Now turn your feet outwards, as far as they will go, and your hands inward, so that your fingers point towards each other. Keep your chest and hips very low to the ground, imagine you have a stick threaded through your shirt from elbow to elbow, and crawl forward using alternating steps of your hands and feet.

Okay . . . (hmph!) . . . still . . . tricky . . . but a bit . . . (hmph!) faster.

Right. And this is how newts, lizards and crocodiles move. Reptiles and amphibians were the first vertebrates with real agility on land, as their multipurpose extremities (limbs) allowed them to crawl, run and even (some of them) jump. But since the shoulders and hips of most* reptiles can't rotate freely and independently (as they do in mammals) they have to wriggle their whole bodies like leggy land-fish in order to move. Which tends to limit their speed and agility.

---

* At least, reptiles still alive today. But many dinosaurs (and other now-extinct prehistoric reptiles) had slightly different hip structures, allowing animals like *Velociraptor* and *Gallimimus* to move terrifyingly fast.

Now let's evolve into mammals.
Go down on all fours – hands and feet – but this time, straighten out your hands and feet so that they point forward. Come up on to your toes, and hold your body a little higher off the ground. Now try moving forward once again. With a bit of practice (and imagination!) you should be able to manage a sinister, cat-like stalk.

Wow. That's much easier. Now I'm walking, rather than crawling.
Right. And that's the advantage mammals have over reptiles. Their shoulders and hips are more free, and their knees and elbows have (over evolutionary time) rotated to face each other, rather than sticking out sideways. Thanks to these changes, mammals became skilled runners, jumpers, dodgers and weavers.

Cool! We mammals *rule*.
And, if you think about it, this is also how we learn to move as we grow from babies to toddlers to children. First, a baby learns to wriggle its spine, so that it can roll over and sit up by itself. Then it learns to crawl, and finally to walk, run and jump. Reptiles, on the other hand, stop developing their movements at the stiff, crawling stage. And though some of them can crawl pretty fast (and a few can even stand up and run), they've got nothing on us mammals – as we've already seen.

That's part of what allowed mammals to survive and replace the dinosaurs as the dominant vertebrates (or back-bone-y things) on the planet. While it was probably an asteroid strike and prolonged climate change that killed off many of the dinosaurs, it was also competition from small, agile, egg-eating mammals that helped to speed up their demise.

Mammals lived alongside dinosaurs?

A few early ones did, yes. But not primates (and certainly not people). Just little shrew-like animals that scampered beneath their feet.* To get a picture of what it was like for mammals back then, imagine a world where a huge lumbering ***Apatosaurus*** ten times the size of elephants might stomp on you at any moment. Where speedy two-legged ***Velociraptors*** might run you down like scaly cheetahs. Or where a terrifying, six-metre-tall ***Tyrannosaurus***s could suddenly bear down on you – its shark-like teeth on display, as it roars and snaps its jaws . . .

Yikes! No wonder those little mammals had to learn to run!

You've got that right!

---

* We know this, because we have actually found fossils of dinosaurs and early shrew-like mammals lying side by side in the same rock layers.

When did fish grow feet – was it before or after they left the water?

Almost certainly **before**, *because without them their air-breathing amphibian descendants couldn't even have got out of the water, let alone enjoyed any advantage of being on the land. In fact, not only frog feet, but also lizard limbs, mouse paws and human hands all evolved from the fleshy fins of fish.*

Are you sure? Couldn't they have just jumped out of the water, and flopped around a bit first?
Okay . . . and then what would they do?

Er . . . I dunno. Snap at a passing insect, then flop their way back into the water?
Well, we've already seen how ill-equipped limbless fish are for moving on land – you tried it yourself, remember? Sharks occasionally beach themselves trying to catch seals in shallow waters, and it doesn't usually work out too well for them. Out of the water, they suffocate in minutes.

Yeah, but sharks can't breathe out of the water, can they? What if the fish evolved lungs, and *then* flopped on to the beach?
Well, whales can breathe out of the water, but beaching doesn't usually go too well for them, either.

Okay, fine. But what if they were smaller, lighter fish that could move themselves about on the shore?

Good point. A few species of fish – called, unsurprisingly, lungfish – have actually evolved primitive lungs, which allow them to survive droughts by burrowing underground and going into a kind of summer hibernation. But to actively hunt, breed or survive for any decent length of time out of the water, the fish would already need some way of lifting and shifting its body on land. Namely, muscular legs. Or, at least, the beginnings of them. And that, it turns out, is almost certainly what the earliest, fishy land-explorers had.

Just a few years ago, fossil-hunting scientists found some incredible evidence of how fish first left the water to become **tetrapods** (four-legged land animals, like frogs, lizards and weasels). It was, quite literally, a fish that could do a push-up.

What? You're joking, right?

Nope. That's exactly what it was. This ancient fossil fish of the *Tiktaalik* genus lived around 375 million years ago. And what makes it special is that its front fins have obvious wrist bones and bony 'fingers', allowing the animal to flex them and lift itself up. While its fins probably weren't strong enough for it to walk, it could nonetheless do something like a push-up to lift its head out of the water – perhaps to catch flying insects.

Experts believe that *Tiktaalik* probably evolved into something like *Acanthostega* or *Icythyostega* (swamp-dwelling animals a bit like giant salamanders, which are the earliest known tetrapods) and – eventually – dinosaurs and other land-based reptiles.

So the muscly foot evolved while the fish still lived underwater?
Exactly.

But why would it need a *foot* underwater?
Possibly to help it scoot along shallow shorelines or riverbeds, as modern manatees (which are, of course, mammals – but you get the idea). And once it was muscly enough to prop the fish up, new possibilities emerged – like finding new food on land, or escaping sharks and other predators in the water. So natural selection happily took care of the rest.

So evolution nicked a fin to make a foot.
Exactly! This 'nicking' of one structure (like a fin) to make another (like a foot) is actually quite common in evolution. It's far easier to adjust an old body part to a new purpose rather than develop a new one from

scratch. The same applies to eyes, wings* and even parts of our brains.

So, after that, fish evolved into amphibians, lizards and mammals?
That's right, they did.

The very first fish were like flattish worms with no jaws, eyes, fins or backbone. Later, they developed into eel-like fish with fleshy fins and sucking mouths, like the **hagfish** and **lampreys** we still see today. After those came fish with bony jaws and fins. It was these bony fish with backbones that later left the seas for life on land, via early fishy tetrapods (or 'fishapods') like *Tiktaalik*. And it was these that ultimately developed into newts, frogs, lizards, dinosaurs, birds, baboons and humans.

With the fishapod's backbone, spinal cord and muscly limbs came mobility, power and strength. And it was this that allowed them to spread into a wider range of successful body types – amphibians, lizards, birds, mammals and more.

So *we* evolved from fish too?
Not right away, but eventually, yes! Fish are our evolutionary ancestors, in that they were the first vertebrates, or backboned animals. And while we didn't descend from exactly the same fish you see around

---

* See 'How did birds learn to fly?' on page 121 for more on this.

you today, we did descend from animals *like* them, which existed many millions of years ago.

In fact, even today, you can still see evidence of this fishy ancestry in our bodies.

Up to the age of four weeks, human and fish embryos look more or less the same. Both have long tails stubby, fin-like limbs and even a set of slots where the gills would go. But after that, human embryos lose their tails as the spine stops developing at the tailbone (or coccyx). Their stubby limb buds grow into arms and legs, and the ancient gill bones become part of the jaw, inner ear and larynx (or voice box).

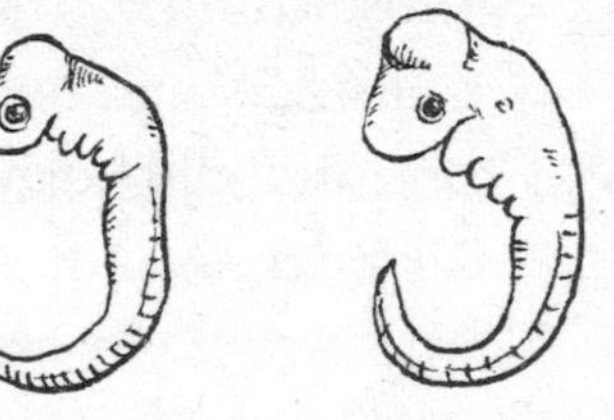

Cool. Bit of a shame we have to lose our gills and tails, though. Having those would be handy for swimming.

Right. Now, when we want to go back under the water, we have to reproduce these fish-like features by strapping on plastic fins, artificial aqualungs and full-on SCUBA gear.

So we spent millions of years evolving ways of leaving the sea to escape being eaten by sharks. Then the first thing we do is jump right back in and start prodding them with sticks.

Pah. Makes you wonder if we've evolved that much after all . . .

How did birds learn to fly?

Little by little, using stubby wings and probably gaining height from trees. We can't say for certain which route early birds took into the air, or even if all birds learned the same way. But scientists think early fliers formed two camps: the daredevil drop-gliders and the ground-running jump-flappers.

Drop-gliders and jump-flappers? Dude – what *are* you talking about?
Sorry – let me explain.

The development of flight has been a mystery since before the time of Darwin. Even after that, all we had was an explanation for how birds might have evolved wings – i.e. bit by bit, from stubby winglets into wide, feathered flying organs. But even Darwin couldn't say for sure which path those early birds took into the sky.

Didn't they just start jumping and flapping?
Okay . . . that's one way it could have happened. But why would they have done that?

I dunno – to catch flying insects or something? Or to escape something chasing them on the ground.
Could be. And, in fact, that's one of the major theories biologists have to explain how birds started flying. Basically it goes like this – birds evolved from

small therapod* dinosaurs. These reptiles were featherless, wingless and ran along the ground on two legs (like an ostrich or roadrunner) to catch prey and escape predators. Then some of these dinosaurs mutated and grew feathers on their bodies and forelimbs. At first these probably just helped to keep them warm. But later they took on a different purpose . . .

Sometimes, when being chased by a predator, these early dino-birds would have to run and jump over obstacles, climb slopes or claw their way up vertical tree trunks to escape. If the mutant, feathered ground-runners flapped their stubby arms as they did this, perhaps they could gain a bit more height, and survive better than animals without these feathered 'winglets'. So, even though these partial wings weren't big or strong enough for them to fly, natural selection would still favour them over no winglets at all. Over time, dinosaurs with bigger, stronger winglets would evolve. Then, eventually, they would develop full-size working wings and learn to leave the ground altogether – as flapping, flying birds.

---

* For more about how and why this happened, see 'Could the dinosaurs ever come back?' on page 151.

That sounds about right to me.
It makes sense to a lot of biologists too. What's more, recently, this theory has been backed up by one scientist working with stubby-winged partridge chicks that were not yet able to fly. In tests, he found that these chicks – if chased towards a slope or vertical wall – will attempt to escape using the running-jumping-flapping method we just described. (He calls it *Wing-assisted Incline Running*, or *WAIR*.)

That's it, then. Sussed.
Not so fast. That's just one theory of how it may have happened. Another is that those early feathered dino-birds started climbing tall trees, launching themselves off and then parachuting or gliding down to the ground.*

Why would they do that?
Again, to find new food sources, or to escape from predators. It might sound like a lot of effort, but other animals – like sugar-gliders and flying squirrels – are already known to do just that. Both these mammals have flaps of skin that stretch from their hands to their feet, forming a thin, fleshy, hang-glider or

---

* The hoatzin, a tropical bird that lives in South American swamps and forests, does something like this even today. Its chicks have claws on the end of their wings, which they use to clamber around in trees before they're properly able to fly. When attacked by snakes or other predators, they drop and glide into underlying water, then use their claws to climb back up again!

parachute that can carry them for long distances in the air.

Flying squirrels climb and drop-glide so that they can search for food among the trees, while staying away from dangerous predators on the ground, such as snakes, weasels, raccoons, bobcats and lynxes.

But can't most of those animals climb trees too?
Right. Which is why it's handy to be able to switch trees in mid-air too. If approached, a flying squirrel will freeze, hoping it won't be spotted. If the snake, weasel or whatever draws closer, the squirrel leaps and glides to the safety of another tree. Most flying squirrels can glide over 30 m (100 feet) between trees,* steering and weaving around them in mid-air to get more distance. Some can also drop their break-away tails to further confuse a predator. Imagine how annoyed you'd be if you were a snake creeping up to attack, and all you ended up with was a mouthful of furry tail and the sight of your prey gliding into the distance . . .

So which one was it, then? Did birds learn to fly like *that*, or by jump-flapping with winglets?
We can't say for sure. There is evidence for both

* The giant Asian flying squirrel and marsupial greater glider can glide over 100 m (300 feet) or more!

theories. The partridge chicks and their wing-assisted running suggest it was jump-flapping. But fossils of the earliest known dino-bird – *Archaeopteryx* – were recently discovered which showed that it had wide clumps of feathers on both its front and hind legs. This suggests that it might have jumped or glided from trees using all four limbs - like a flying squirrel.

In any case, birds have come a long way since then. While many other animals have evolved many types of flight, birds are definitely the most accomplished aeronauts. (See the quiz overleaf to find out more.)

Either way, I definitely wanna try that tree-gliding thing. If a flying squirrel can do it, then so can I!

Well, before you go taping bedsheets to your wrists and ankles, you should probably know this – birds and flying squirrels have much lighter bones and muscles than you do. Any attempt to fly in the same way will probably end up with a trip to the hospital, accompanied by flashing lights and angry parents.

Boo. That's no fun.

Cheer up. You could always take up hang-gliding.

Oh, yeah! And for added effect, I could get my mate to dress up like a weasel and chase me off the edge . . .

Each to their own, I suppose . . .

Bird-brainy

Try this bird-themed quiz to test your knowledge of our flying feathered friends

1. The largest living bird in the world is the

a Golden eagle
b Ostrich
c Andean condor
d Elephant bird

2. How many times a second does the average hummingbird beat its wings?

a 1–5 times
b 5–10 times
c 10–100 times
d 100–1,000 times

3. The fastest flying bird in the world is the peregrine falcon. How fast can it go in a full, vertical dive?

a 50 mph
b 100 mph
c 150 mph
d Over 200 mph

4. Which of the following can NO known species of bird do?

a Run
b Swim
c Talk
d Turn its head through 360°
e Echolocate
f Use tools

(*answers on page 208*)

If sharks are so deadly, how come they haven't eaten all the other fish by now?

Because, deadly as sharks are, they couldn't eat them all even if they tried. Smaller fish breed much faster than sharks, and for a whole host of reasons they're slippery, elusive prey. And, besides, if they did eat all the other fish, they'd have nothing much left to live on.

How's that, then? I thought sharks were, you know, right at the top of the food chain.

They are. But in order to stay there they need every animal (and plant) in the chain beneath them. Land-based predators like lions depend on large quantities of antelopes and grasses to support them.* In ocean food chains, the same applies. Predatory sharks depend on smaller fish, sea plants and algae further down the chain. If they ate too many fish (or if an area is over-fished by humans), then the sharks in that area will start to die off. So just as with lions and antelopes, there's a natural balance between predators and prey.

That said, there's a big difference between antelopes and small fish.

---

* For more about food chains, see 'If one species owned the planet, which one would it be?' on page 69.

Duhhhh. Of course there is. Antelopes have legs, for starters.
Er . . . right. But, *apart* from that, fish also breed faster. Much faster. Antelope give birth to just one or two young per year. But the typical fish lays *thousands* of eggs (a female salmon lays 4–6 million in one spawning!). And, while only a tenth of these may survive to become adult fish, that's still hundreds or thousands of new ones entering the food chain every year. Even if sharks *tried* to eat them all, they could never hope to keep up. This, it turns out, is part of the fish's clever survival strategy.

Pah. That doesn't sound very clever to me. That still means loads of stupid fish get eaten.
Well, they have other ways of not becoming shark-food too. And maybe fish aren't as stupid as you think . . .

Fish were the first animals with a separate central nervous system (or brain), and the first to develop specialized sense organs that taste, smell and hear.

Fish have ears?
Not ears like ours, no. (That would look pretty weird.)

But they do have organs for sensing sounds and pressure changes, which is pretty much all an ear is. These are called **lateral line organs**, and they run from the fish's head all the way down the sides of its body. You can actually see this line on most fish. With these, it can detect sound waves and pressure changes in the water, like those caused by an approaching motorboat, swimmer or shark. With its lateral line organs, the fish will usually *hear* or *feel* the movement of a predator long before it sees one. So any loud noises or sudden movements in the water near a fish's body will trigger a **startle reflex**. With this, the fish curls up its body – turning its head away from the noise or threat – and swims off at a random angle.* (Interestingly, as a hangover from our fishy past, humans still show this startle reflex when we hear a loud noise or get surprised by a sudden movement. Our spines curl up, our heads turn away from the threat and – usually – we run for it.) These 'listening' organs also allow fish to automatically sense the movement of other fish nearby, allowing them to move together as one, in a **shoal**.

But how would that help them survive? Doesn't that just put them all in the same place, making them easier for sharks to scoff?

Actually, shoaling makes it very hard for sharks (plus

---

* This is also why it's so difficult to catch a fish with your hands, and we're forced to use nets or hooks instead.

dolphins, seals, penguins or anything else) to snap up individual fish, because the movement confuses them. Think of those game shows where they put the contestant in a big glass tank with a high-powered fan and paper money flying all over the place. All they have to do is grab the money to keep it, but often they fail to catch more than a few notes, as they can't decide which ones to grab at. You could call it the 'spoilt for choice' defence.

That said, sharks – and their cousins, rays – have a few tricks up their sleeves too, and certainly keep the little fish on their toes. Or fins, rather.

Tricks like what?

In addition to those pressure-sensing lateral-line organs, many sharks have evolved special electricity-sensing organs in their noses, called **ampullary** organs. They can use these to pick up the tiny bio-electric fields given off by twitching fish muscles, allowing them to locate prey in complete darkness, or even fish buried in sand or silty seabeds.

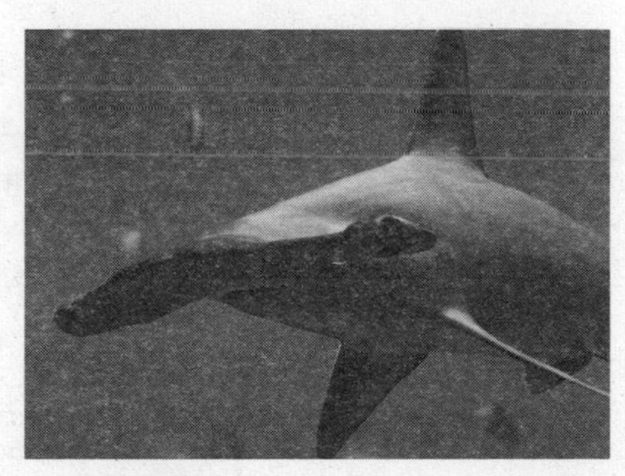

Hammerhead sharks are especially good at this. In fact, that's the main reason why their strange, flat heads are shaped the way they are – they are like huge satellite dishes, picking up electric signals from below their bodies. When hunting, they sweep their heads from left to right like metal detectors, scanning the sandy seabed for invisible, twitching morsels.

Cool! Can they zap things with their electric heads, too?

No, but their cousins, torpedo rays, can. Sharks and rays are part of the same class of ancient fish, called the **Elasmobranchii**. You've probably heard of the venomous stingray, which has evolved a single venomous spine for attack and defence. Well, torpedo rays went one better. They evolved a pair of electric organs* to stun prey and deter predators. These organs, stuffed with electricity-storing cells called electrocytes, sit either side of its head. When it attacks a fish, the ray glides above it and lets rip with both batteries – shocking and paralyzing its prey with up to 4 kW of electric power. If attacked by a predator, they do the same.

Superb! Could they, like, zap you to death?

Probably not, as their zapping charge has a high current but a low voltage.** Still, it'd be enough to give you

---

* As in, 'body organs that make electricity', not that cheesy electric-piano thing your grandad probably plays. Torpedo rays would have difficulty carting a pair of those about.

** South American electric eels, however, can generate a charge of up to 400 volts – enough to kill an adult human.

a very nasty shock. Literally. Most rays (including stingrays and the enormous manta rays) aren't much of a danger to people. And, for that matter, neither are most sharks.

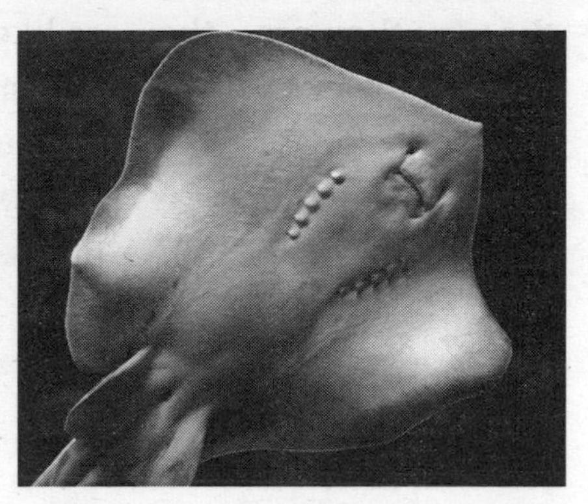

But I thought sharks ate people?

Not really. Or, at least, not often. Some of them, it's true, regularly bite people. But they don't often stick around to finish you off. Even the famous 'man-eating' great white shark (species name *Carcharodon carcharias*, which, inventively, means 'sharky-shark') doesn't bite more than ten or twenty people a year, worldwide. And most of those unfortunate swimmers and surfers actually *survive* the attacks - only a handful of people actually *die* in shark attacks each year.

Still, I wouldn't want to be one of 'em.

Me neither. Great whites have up to 3,000 razor-sharp teeth – arranged in several rows that replace each other as they're blunted or fall out. Each one is up to 8 cm (3 inches) long – about the same length as your index finger. The animal itself grows up to 5 m (16 feet) long – bigger than most three-seater sofas.

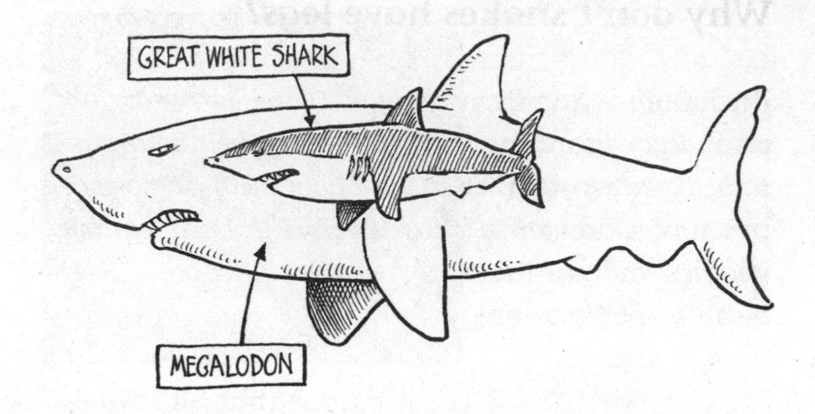

Imagine something *that* big bearing down on you with a mouthful of butcher knives!

But get this – in prehistoric times, there was a shark roaming the oceans called *Carcharodon megalodon*. It's name means 'big-toothed shark', and this is something of an understatement. It went extinct around 50 million years ago, soon after most of the dinosaurs, and its teeth (found fossilized, all around the world) were over 18 cm (6 inches) long.

Biologists reckon that this would make its *mouth* measure over 3 m (10 feet) across, and its body over 16 m (50 feet) long. That would make it about the same size as a single-decker *bus*.

Yikes! I'm glad *that* one's no longer around!

Yep. Not sure how many surfers and SCUBA divers would be left, otherwise . . .

Why don't snakes have legs?

Because they lost them! Around 60 million years ago, many leggy lizard species began losing their limbs, as it turned out they were better off without them. Some ended up with four shrunken limbs, others with back legs only, and still others with no legs at all. The latter group, eventually, became snakes.

They *lost* them? You're telling me that all snakes *had* legs once?
That's right, they did.

But how could they just lose them?
Well, it wasn't quite like forgetting your lunchbox or your school bag. They didn't just leave their burrows one morning, slither off to the mouse hunt, then suddenly stop and think, Oops – I forgot my legs. As with most things in evolution, it didn't happen overnight. Just as it took thousands of years for fish to evolve legs (and become lizards) in the first place, it probably took thousands more for snakes to *un*-evolve (or *de*-evolve) them.

Animals can *un*-evolve things too?

Well, technically it's all just *evolving*. But if you mean 'can they lose features they gained' through evolution, then yes – they can and they do. Snakes aren't the only example of this, either. Whales and dolphins evolved from animals with legs too, but lost them when they returned to the sea. And other animals have gained (and later lost) tails, fur, feathers . . . even eyes and ears. It all depends on what's needed to survive, and what's not. Natural selection doesn't care what the animal looks like. Some live, some die, some breed, others fail, and in the end the best-adapted animals survive, regardless of what they may look like (or whether they quite *enjoyed* having legs, thank you very much).

So how did that happen with snakes?

The four-legged, reptilian ancestors of snakes were burrowing lizards living alongside the dinosaurs. They lived in the Cretaceous period, over 65 million years ago. These particular lizards specialized in slipping through soils, sands, swamp reeds and thick grasses to find their prey and escape dangerous predators. Once they had adapted to that lifestyle, it soon became clear that limbs were more of a hindrance than a help.

Why's that?

Well, imagine trying to crawl through a narrow tunnel wearing a big backpack that sticks out on each

side. When you're living and hunting in narrow burrows and openings, anything left sticking out from your body makes it more difficult to move quickly. For these prehistoric snakey lizards, that could mean the difference between lunch and no lunch, between being captured and escaping to safety.

Okay. That makes sense.

Now through natural changes (or mutations) in their DNA, a few mutant lizards with smaller (or reduced) limbs appeared. When they did, they survived and reproduced better than those with more sticky-out appendages. And so, over time, two new groups of reptiles emerged in the animal kingdom.

Skinks, of the family **Scincidae**, include lizards with shrunken limbs or those with one pair of limbs (either forelimbs or hindlimbs) only. Skinks are actually the largest and most widespread family of lizards on the planet. So for a lizard, it seems, having legs ain't all it's cracked up to be!

Meanwhile, a whole new order of legless reptiles – the **snakes**, or **Squamata** – emerged alongside them. And they turned out to be a big success too. There are now over 3,000 species of snake in the world, including burrowing snakes, sea snakes, tree snakes, even flying snakes!*

* Which don't actually fly, but can leap and glide between trees by flattening their bodies. Which is still a pretty nifty trick.

That's pretty crazy. So how do we know all this? How do we know snakes didn't just evolve from some legless animal in the first place? Like a worm or something.

Partly from the fossil record, where we find ancient, land-based reptiles on the verge of losing their legs. And partly from living snake species as, believe it or not, some of them still have hip bones and leg bones tucked away beneath their scaly skin!

No way!

It's true. The so-called **primitive snakes,*** like pythons and boa constrictors, have small pelvises (or hip bones) and femurs (or thigh bones) attached to their spines, which are easily seen on X-rays or complete snake skeletons. This proves, once and for all, that the ancestors of snakes had legs. Unless, of course, you think pythons and boas are in the process of growing them back.

Wow. Leggy snakes. I always thought snakes had, you know, always been legless. I mean, that's what makes a snake a snake, isn't it?

---

* Although I wouldn't call them that to their faces. After all – they're *huge*.

Partly, yes. But snakes have a couple of other unique features among reptiles too, aside from their famous legless . . . er . . . -ness. They also have hollow fangs, which some species of snake use to inject venom as they bite. And they're the only vertebrates that swallow their prey whole.

Yeah – why *do* they do that?
Do what – use venomous bites, or swallow things whole?

Both.
Okay – well, the venom evolved from simple saliva or digestive juice, slowly turning from an acid to a blood-clotting or nerve-paralyzing poison. Again, it started with chance mutations, and over time the snakes with more toxic saliva, unsurprisingly, found it easier to kill prey. In particular, it allowed them to take bigger and bigger prey – biting the animal once and then retreating to a safe distance while it succumbed to the poison. Over time, most snakes also evolved larger fangs (all the better to bite you with) with grooves or hollows running down the back of the fangs, which helped to deliver the venom more efficiently from the salivary glands.

A few species of snake, of course, took a different route to deadliness. Pythons, anacondas and boa constrictors simply grew into huge-muscled monsters, large and powerful enough to coil around their prey and squeeze them into suffocation.

But, in any case, now these snakes had a problem. They could kill animals (like rats, birds and frogs – although some can take animals as large as pigs and deer!) that were far larger than their own heads. But, without large powerful jaws and teeth for slicing and chewing them up, how would they go about swallowing something that large? And without suffocating in the process.

So how do they manage it?

They dislocate their faces. Or, more specifically, their jaws and skull bones. Unlike mammals, snakes have over seventeen flexible connections in their skulls and jaws, all held together by ligaments (by comparison, humans have one – the hinge between a solid skull and a single jawbone).

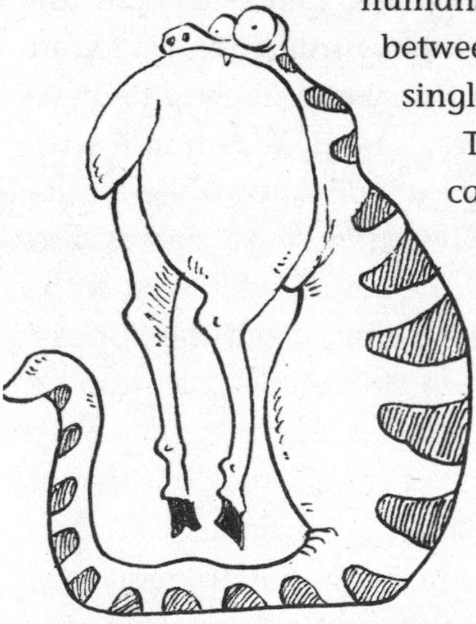

This means the snake can fold its skull practically in half, and move the left and right side of its jaws independently in order to 'walk' its mouth and head over the outsized body of its prey. As it does so, it also slides its windpipe forward (and under the huge, meaty morsel in its mouth) to snatch breaths – a bit like snorkelling. Imagine swallowing an entire hamburger (or just an apple) without chewing. Well, snakes manage to gulp down things far larger relative to the size of their bodies – equivalent to you gulping down a whole turkey or goat.

Gross! . . . But also *brilliant*! I wish *I* could do that.
Don't even think about it. We mammals evolved our teeth for a reason. And since you can't move your jaw, skull or windpipe about, you'd choke to death in minutes trying to swallow even a small morsel of food. People choke to death every year on peanuts. So listen to your mum when she tells you to 'chew your food properly'.

Aside from that, it'd be pretty disgusting for all your friends to watch. I know I wouldn't want to sit next to 'snake boy' at lunchtime . . .

Scary snake facts

- The largest snake in the world is the reticulated python, which reaches lengths of over 10 m (30 feet) – about the same length as the average passenger bus.

- The deadliest snake in the world is not the king cobra (found in Asia), nor the dreaded diamondback rattlesnake (found in North America). It's the rare fierce snake, native to central Australia. Just 100 g of its venom is powerful enough to kill 100 adult humans, or over 250,000 mice.

- The smallest snake in the world is a species of threadsnake called *Leptotyphlops*. Recently discovered on the Caribbean island of Barbados, it reaches an adult length of just 10 cm (4 inches), and has been nicknamed the microsnake.

- Jumping vipers can leap up to 1 m (3 feet) off the ground, and at least two species of tree snake can fly (or, rather, glide) by flattening their ribcages and flinging themselves out of trees.

- The spitting cobra can 'spit' its poison out at its prey over distances of up to 2 m, and usually aims for the eyes . . .

Why are frogs always gulping and croaking?

They gulp as they breathe, because – unlike us – they have to force air into their lungs by swallowing it. The croaking is actually frog song. They use it to attract mates, mark their territory or just chat about the weather!

Frogs swallow air to breathe? Wait a minute – do frogs have lungs, or gills, or what?
Both. And most of them can breathe through their skin too.

What?
It's true. Frogs, newts and salamanders make up the larger part of the class **Amphibia** – the first group of vertebrates that evolved to live both in and out of the water. (The word actually means 'both lives' in Greek, which nicely describes their habitat-hopping habits.) Within this class, newts and salamanders form the order **Caudata** (meaning, 'tailed ones'), while frogs and toads are of the order **Anura** (or 'tail-less ones'). You can probably guess why.

Frogs and toads breathe through their skin and gills as young tadpoles, living solely in the water. But as they develop legs they also develop air sacs, or *lungs*. In adult frogs and toads, these take over most of the breathing duties – although they also continue to breathe through their skin. This is part of the reason

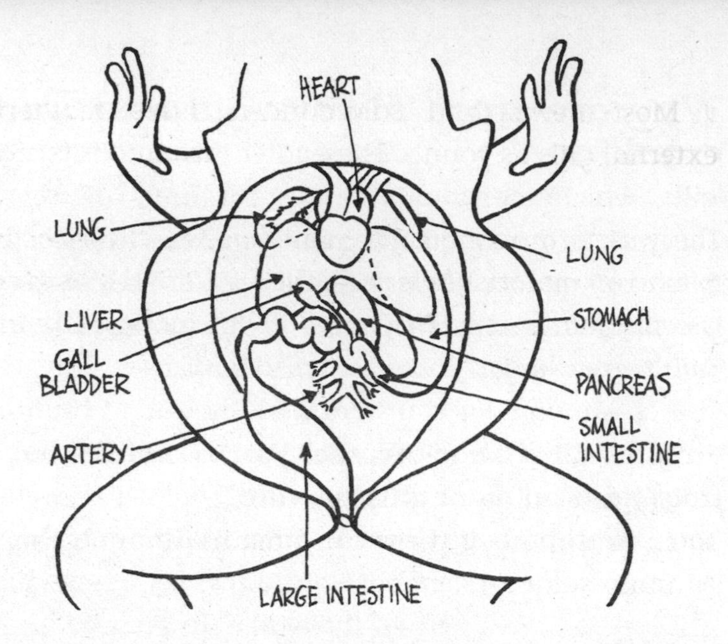

why frogs and toads tend to live in wet or watery places, like ponds, rivers and rainforests – they have to keep their skin moist so that oxygen can dissolve into it from the air. The other reason, of course, is that most* frogs and toads lay their eggs in the water.

What about newts – can they breathe through their skin too?

With newts and salamanders, it's a bit more complicated. While pretty much all of them can breathe through their skin, some have lungs, while others do not.

---

* I say 'most', because not all of them do. The female Argentinian Darwin's frog (*Rhinoderma darwinii*), for example, lays its eggs in the forest, and the male picks them up and carries them around in his chin (or vocal) pouch! The eggs hatch into tadpoles inside, and the father spits them out into the water when they're half grown.

Most newts and salamanders have feathery external gills as young. These later turn into internal gills, which the adult animals continue to use in the water throughout life. One species, the ghostly Mexican **axolotl**, keeps its feathery external gills even as an adult, so it spends its whole life looking like an adult-sized baby. (To get some idea of how unusual this is – imagine if you were a six-foot adult human with the same long body, short limbs and huge bald, outsized head you had as a baby. *That's* how weird the axolotl probably looks to other salamanders!)

Some salamanders develop lungs, lose their gills and yet remain living in the water. To breathe, they have to surface for air like coastal dolphins. Others, meanwhile, lack both lungs and gills, and spend their whole lives on land, breathing only through their slimy skin. In a dry spell, these guys are really in trouble – because if their skin dries out they can't breathe, and quickly suffocate.

All of these strange and wonderful habits, of course, offer clues as to how these animals evolved. Amphibians have the longest history of all vertebrate animals. Modern frogs, toads, newts and salamanders all evolved from fleshy, lobe-finned fish over 200 million years ago, just as the dinosaurs were taking over the land.* Reptiles and mammals evolved from

---

* In fact, at least one biologist has suggested that frogs evolved their high-speed hopping in order to escape hungry dinosaurs!

a group of land-based, newt-like animals with lungs, that started spending more and more of their life cycles on land.

Good job too.
What do you mean?

Well, if it had been from one of the other groups, we'd have to breathe through our skin instead!
Actually, animals as large as us could *never* breathe through our skins alone. Our larger bodies need more oxygen than smaller animals, so we need a larger surface area to exchange oxygen and waste gases. Our lungs, thankfully, provide that extra area for us. If you unfolded all the tiny branching tubes and sacs inside our lungs, it would have roughly the same surface area as a tennis court.

Yeah – and if we did have to breathe through our skins, we wouldn't be able to wear clothes, or we'd suffocate. So everyone would be in the nude all the time. Even your parents. Urrghhh!
Er . . . right.

So are frog lungs the same as ours, then?
Not quite. Ours differ from those of frogs and other air-breathing amphibians in that we have **lung muscles** – the most important being the large, flat diaphragm muscle that sits beneath them. With this,

we can expand the twin air sacs in our chests to draw in air.

A frog, however, lacks these lung muscles. So it uses its mouth and throat muscles instead. To take a breath, the frog sucks air into its closed mouth through its nostrils, and then swallows the air to force it into the lungs. It does this by lowering and raising the floor of its mouth, which also makes the frog look like it's 'gulping' or swallowing something every few seconds.

Well, that explains all the gulping. But what about the croaking?

In a way, that's tied to the breathing. Many frog species have a large, stretchy vocal sac below their mouths. This sac can expand like a balloon and draw in *extra* air when the frog takes a deep breath in. By contracting muscles in the sac, the frog can shift the air to and from the lungs via the throat, vibrating its vocal cords on the way past. This is what makes the croak or 'ribbit' sound frogs are so famous for.*

But by contracting and vibrating their vocal sacs and vocal cords in different ways, different species

---

* In fact, very few species of frog actually go 'ribbit'. The reason why we link this sound to frogs is because one common frog species in the USA, in California, makes it. Sound engineers working on early Hollywood movies began recording sound clips of local frogs, for movie 'background' noises in films featuring swamps or jungles. And the same clips have been reused for years. So most of us think frogs go 'ribbit' because that's what *movie* frogs sound like!

Animal categories

Test your vertebrate knowledge by naming a species for each starting letter.

The first line (all vertebrates starting with the letter 'F') has been done for you. Now fill in the blank lines by naming an animal starting with the letter indicated for each of the five major categories of back-boned animals.

Letter	Fish	Amphibian
F	Flounder	Frog
S		
T	Tuna	
C		Cane toad
R	Ray	
G		
A		

Now play against your friends by naming a letter each round, and seeing who can think of the most animals (of any category) beginning with that letter in thirty seconds. You can either jot them down on paper, or – if you're in a car, on a journey – just shout them out and keep score that way. But don't shout too loud – you'll annoy your parents. Unless of course you get them to join in too . . .

Reptile	Bird	Mammal
Frilled lizard	Fulmar	Fox
Skunk		
		Thrush
		Racoon
	Gannet	
Axolotl	Alligator	

of frog can produce hugely different sounds instead. Some sound like bells, gongs or whistles – others sound like dripping taps, burps, car horns or clarinets! In the rainforests of Brazil or Borneo, there are so many frog sounds at night that it sounds like a full froggy orchestra is playing, all night long.

Except you don't get many orchestras with whistlers and burpers sitting next to the violins and clarinets.
True. But if you did they could play a little Toad-zart, perhaps.

Groan.
Or perhaps some Newt-hoven.

Good grief.
Dun-dun-dun-DUNNNN (ribbit).

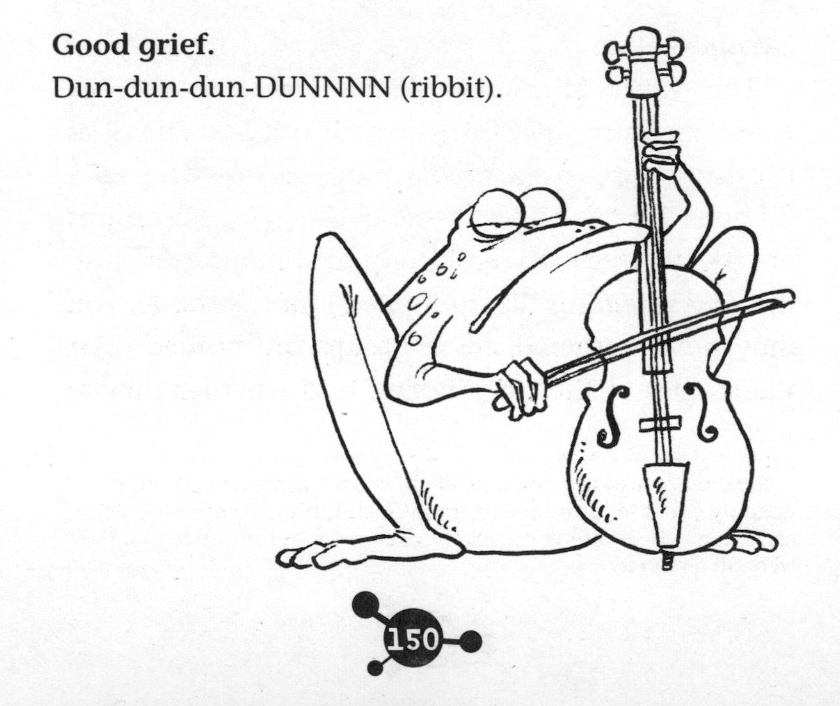

Could the dinosaurs ever come back?

Some of them never left! Many small dinosaurs didn't actually go extinct. They evolved into the birds you see around you every day. As for the others, it seems unlikely. It is currently impossible to clone them, Jurassic Park*-style, from ancient DNA. And, even if we could, the modern world would be a tough place for a dinosaur to live.*

They never left? You mean they're *still here*?
In a way, yes. You see, not all of the dinosaurs died. And many of the large reptiles that *did* die were not actually dinosaurs, anyway.

Eh?
Let me explain.

The word 'dinosaur' comes from two Greek words meaning 'fearfully great lizard'.* It describes two major groups of reptile that lived between 205 million and 65 million years ago. These two groups are the *ornithischian* (or 'bird-hipped') dinosaurs and the *saurischian* (or 'lizard-hipped') dinosaurs. As you may have gathered, these groups are named after the shapes of their hip bones, and whether they're

---

* Most books usually translate *dinosaur* as 'terrible lizard', but it's actually closer to 'awesome lizard'. Which I think fits them better, anywhere. They weren't all terrible, but as far as I'm concerned they were all *awesome*.

shaped more like a bird's (tilted backwards) or like a lizard's (tilted forward). Got it?

Got it.

Good. Now the **ornithischian** dinos were all plant-eaters, and included the armour-plated stegosaurs and ankylosaurs, the three-horned *Triceratops*, the kangaroo-like ornithopods (the most common being the elephant-sized *Iguanodon*) and many others.

As for the **saurischian** dinos, these fell into two main groups. The first were the huge, four-legged, plant-eating **sauropods**. This group includes *Diplodocus*, *Apatosaurus* and the immense Brachiosaurus, which was 25 m (80 feet) long, and weighed up to 90 tonnes (or the same as fifteen to twenty adult elephants). The second **saurischian** group are the two-legged, meat-eating **therapods**. These include the fast-moving *Velociraptor* and the terrifying *Tyrannosaurus rex*, and the even larger (and more terryifying) *Gigantosaurus*. Remember these guys. We'll come back to them.

But the dinosaurs weren't the only large reptiles around. In the air, there were the flying **pterosaurs** (including the famous *Pterodactyl*). In the oceans, the Nessie-like **plesiosaurs** and dolphin-like **ichthyosaurs**. And on land, the sail-backed *Dimetrodon* and others.

So they're not dinosaurs, then?

Nope. Most people mistake them for dinosaurs, but technically they're not. They're just large prehistoric

reptiles. In any case, together, these all-powerful reptiles ruled the Earth for over 150 million years. But sadly most of them went the same way at the end of the Cretaceous period, around 65 million years ago.

So what happened? How did they die?

As far as we can tell, most of the dinosaurs were offed by a whole series of events that happened during the late Cretaceous period. This included massive volcanic eruptions, a number of impacts from enormous asteroids (one of which smashed into the ocean close to the coast of Mexico), and a period of rapid, catastrophic climate change.

Whatever the case, by the end of the Cretaceous period, most of the dinosaurs – along with four-fifths of the world's plants, a third of its mammals and up to 65% of all animal species worldwide – were gone. However, they didn't disappear at once. Some struggled on for thousands of years, and while pretty much all of the ornithischians went extinct, a good number of the **saurischian** therapod dinosaurs survived and evolved.

Wait a minute – that's the group that includes *Velociraptors* and *Tyrannosaurus rex*, right?
Right.

Wicked! So where are they?
Sadly, the largest therapods all died. But some of the smaller ones evolved feathers and, eventually, wings.* So while most of the prehistoric world's large reptiles died, a good number of the **saurischians** live on through their modern descendants – birds.

Really? Like chickens, and sparrows, and ostriches?
Really. If you think about it, it isn't such a stretch. Just watch a chicken or ostrich walk some time. Look at its scaly legs and clawed feet, imagine it without feathers, and bang – there it is . . . a mini *Velociraptor*.

Yeah, yeah. But a chicken-sized dinosaur is hardly very scary, is it?
Up until the seventeenth century, you could have seen a much larger, scarier dino-descendant on the island of Madagascar. The 3 m (10-foot) tall, flight-

---

* You can learn more about these early dino-birds in 'How did birds learn to fly?' on page 121.

less **elephant bird** was about half the size of a *Stegosaurus*, but still big enough to maim or kill you with a well-aimed kick. Sadly, this wasn't enough to protect it from human hunters, who chased it to extinction around 400 years ago.

Seeing one of those would be pretty smart, I s'pose. But why did all the big ones have to die? I mean, they were *so* cool. And if other big lizards like crocodiles are as old as the dinosaurs, how come the dinosaurs died but *they* didn't?

We don't know for certain, but it's fairly safe to say sharks and crocs were somehow better adapted to survive the changes that happened around 65 million years ago, when most of the dinosaurs disappeared. It may have been to do with size and competition. Larger animals need larger food supplies, so perhaps reptiles larger than sharks and crocodiles had a harder time finding enough food.

Large reptiles also find it more difficult to regulate their body temperatures (which is why crocodiles and alligators only live in tropical or sub-tropical areas). Without fur or feathers, the larger dinosaurs may have had more trouble – compared to crocs and smaller reptiles – in keeping warm during the colder winters that followed the asteroid strike, volcanic eruptions and climate change. This, then, might also explain why some of the smaller ones evolved feathers and became birds – not, in the beginning, for *flight* . . . but for *warmth*.

Whatever the reason, we do know this: if the dinosaurs were to come back today, they'd find a very different world to the one they evolved to live in – a world in which it would be very tough for them to survive and thrive.

But dinosaurs are *well* tough! *Nothing* could beat a dinosaur. They're tougher than anything!

Maybe. But, then again, maybe not. For one thing, they evolved and conquered the Earth largely in the absence of mammals. But when the dinosaurs died off, the mammals filled all their niches and replaced them in the food chains. Left to compete with ruthless, egg-eating mammals today, they might not do so well.

Nor are dinosaurs tougher than the *climate*. During the late Cretaceous period when the dinosaurs last lived, the climate was much warmer. There were no ice caps at the poles, and dinosaurs migrated back and forth between warm, wet North America, Africa, Asia and Europe, and a pleasantly cool Russia, Canada and Greenland. Sixty-five million years later, the air is thinner, the plants are different and the world – despite steadily increasing temperatures thanks to global warming – is generally a lot cooler.

It was a rapidly changing climate and environment that spelled the end of the dinosaurs in the first place. Thrust them back into the world now and the chances are they wouldn't last too long.

All right – but *what if* we *could* clone them? And *what if* global warming heated up the world so much that it was better suited to dinosaurs than mammals? And *what if* they busted out of all the science labs and scoffed all the mammals, including us? *Then* would dinosaurs rule the world again?
That's a lot of *what ifs* . . . but it's possible, I suppose.

That's good enough for me!
Wait a minute – do you actually *want* to be eaten by a dinosaur?

Who cares? Dinosaurs RULE! RRRRRAAAAAAAA!
(Sigh.)

Dino facts

- The vast majority of dinosaurs were herbivores (plant-eaters), rather than carnivores.
- The famous *Tyrannosarus rex* was not, in fact, the largest carnivorous dinosaur. The largest known *T. rex* measured 13 m (42 feet) long, and weighed over 6 tonnes. But at 18 m (60 feet) long and weighing in at almost 10 tonnes, the terrifying sail-backed

Spinosaurus would have towered over it. Luckily for *T. rex*, *Spinosaurus* lived thousands of years earlier, so they never met.

- Many dinosaurs were feathered, and some were probably quite brightly coloured, like modern-day peacocks and parrots.
- Male *Velcociraptors* had feathery 'top-knot' hair-styles, which they probably used to attract picky females.

6.
We Mighty Mammals

Let me tell you a story . . . The story of a great battle.

The time – the Cretaceous period, over 65 million years ago.

The place – planet Earth, but not as we know it.

In the northern hemisphere, Europe, Greenland and North America sat much closer together than they are now, and were joined by bridges of low-lying land. In the southern hemisphere, Africa and South America were just a few hundred miles apart, as the floor of the Atlantic had yet to widen out and form a wide ocean between them. Australia sat pinned to Antarctica, and India floated in the yawning Pacific off the east coast of Africa, just beginning its shift northwards to plough into Asia, forming the vast Himalayan mountain range . . .

For over 150 million years, ravenous reptiles – large and small – had ruled the Earth. Long-necked plesiosaurs swam in the oceans, bat-winged pterosaurs swooped through the skies, while huge brachiosaurs and terrifying tyrannosaurs stomped the land.

At their feet scampered the tiny, insignificant mammals. No larger than weasels or rats, the mammals had been scavenging plants, insects and the meaty kills of the great lizards for millennia – the underlings of the prehistoric world. But soon this was all to change . . .

Great volcanoes erupted, spewing fire and sulphur into the atmosphere. Huge boulders rained down from the skies, smashing into the Earth and throwing up vast dust clouds that blotted out the sun for months at a time. The climate shifted, bringing colder, dryer winters that killed off all but the hardiest animals.

The Great Lizards were tested, and most struggled to survive. The larger ones fell, and the largest fell hardest of all. But at their feet the mammals found ways to survive and thrive, and a new world order was beginning. In a harsh, changing world, the remaining reptiles and the rising ranks of mammals fought a final battle for dominion over the land.

In the end, the mammals emerged victorious and spread throughout the world, ever to rule the reptiles as kings among the vertebrates. As a new era began, huge, hairy mammals stomped the earth, while their smaller, more agile cousins hunted the plains, stalked the forests, swung through the trees and even took to the skies. The reptiles shrank and scampered into burrows and slithered at the feet of their new rulers, leaving only a few, large, crocodilian remnants of their former glory to lurk in rivers . . . mumbling about the 'good old days' . . . snapping at the mammals in revenge. Small skirmishes were continued by the snakes and others continued, but it was no use – the battle was won. The mammals had inherited the Earth, and the Age of Reptiles was no more.

THE END

Or, rather, The Beginning. Because THAT, my friends, is how we mighty mammals came to be the great, world-altering class of animals we are today – from the tiniest shrew to the tallest giraffe, the strongest elephant, the most enormous whale and the cleverest human.*

Now, together, let's take our final trip, to meet the rulers of the vertebrate world.

---

* *Me*. Obviously. :o)

If all mammals make milk, do kangaroos make milkshakes?

Kangaroo mothers do make milk, but sadly no amount of hopping and bouncing will turn it into a milkshake for their young joeys. That said, plain old mammalian milk is pretty amazing stuff all by itself. It was one of three secret weapons that allowed mammals to outwit reptiles, and replace them as the most powerful vertebrates on the planet.

No milkshakes, then? Boo. Pity. I thought maybe it could lob a couple of strawberries or bananas into the pouch, and . . .

Sadly, no. Aside from the fact that strawberries and bananas don't grow in the hot, dry Australian Outback, kangaroo milk isn't made in the pouch, anyway. (That's just where the joeys receive it). Nice idea, though.

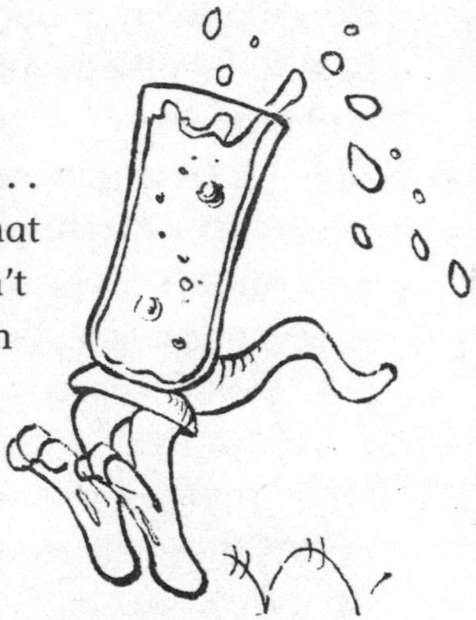

Sigh. All right, then – what's so great about plain old mammal's milk?

Being mammals ourselves, we tend to take milk for granted. But, if you think about it, it's truly amazing stuff. It's a delicious, nutritious, mobile food – one that baby mammals can survive on for months or even years, in the absence of *anything* else. Along with a few other special features, the ability to produce milk is part of what *defines* mammals. It's also part of what gave mammals the edge in that age-old battle with their prehistoric rivals – the reptiles – that we just heard about in the intro to this chapter.

Yeah, that was very exciting and all, but I didn't quite get one thing.
What was that?

How did the mammals manage to survive and beat the reptiles, when they started out so small and puny?
Ahh – good question. With new tactics for survival. Which is where kangaroo pouches and mammalian milk come in . . .

Mammals, you see, were the first animals to give birth to live young – rather than lay eggs. Reptiles, by contrast, lay eggs. In general, laying eggs means staying put, or nesting, and reptile parents have to protect their defenceless, immobile young while they slowly develop inside the eggs, or risk losing them to egg-eating animals. Even the dinosaurs had to do this. Part of what finished them off was probably small mammals eating their eggs.

But mammals found a way around this weakness. Giving birth to live young allowed mammals to stay on the move, taking their weak, toddling (but mobile) babies with them as they looked for food or hid from predators. Some mammals (the marsupials) went one better by evolving pouches in which to keep their babies. This allowed them to reproduce *faster*, by giving birth to babies that were little more than embryos, then safely transporting and nursing them in the pouch until they were big enough to walk and follow their mother. This is why kangaroos – along with wallabies, possums* and other marsupial mammals – have pouches.

Okay, so pouches were a plus for some mammals. But how did milk help?

Milk enabled mammals to feed their weak, undeveloped, vulnerable young while living life on the move. As embryos, egg-laying animals feed off the nutrients in the egg's yolk. If they're lucky – and the egg isn't scoffed first – they hatch as weak, puny babies. They then mature slowly into adults, largely unguarded by their parents, who have to spend most of their time away, looking for food. (Just think of a

* Some possums even have *waterproof* pouches, which they can snap shut while swimming to keep their young safe and dry inside.

bird leaving its nest to fetch worms. Not all reptiles look after their young that well – many abandon their young soon after hatching – but you get the idea.) This leaves the babies at risk of attack, even after they're born.

Mammals, on the other hand, have milk-producing mammary glands (or at least the females do). This turns them into mobile food dispensers, churning out litres and litres of high-protein, high-vitamin, 'super-gro' baby food on the move. This constant supply of liquid wonder-grub allows the babies to grow and mature very quickly, making them more likely to survive to adulthood.

Kangaroo mothers, amazingly, can produce three different types of milk – with different amounts of fat and nutrients – to feed joeys of different ages at the same time. One tiny, day-old joey may be suckling one type of milk deep inside the pouch, while another three-month-old joey hops beneath the mother to receive a different milk formula from another teat. So kangaroo mums have milk-making down to a fine art. But all mammals make milk, and all of them have benefited from the security it provides for their young.

So that's what allowed the mammals to win out over the reptiles? Milk power?

Mostly, yes. But mammals also had one more trick up their sleeves. Or, rather, on their bodies.

Hair.

Hair?

Yep – hair. With very few exceptions, all mammals are hairy or furry. But there's not an amphibian or reptile in the world with a patch of the stuff, not even the hairy frog. They have scales instead, and lack the special cells from which hair follicles grow. Hair not only makes mammals look nice and cuddly, it also keeps them warm and cosy. Hair – and the thick mats of it we call *fur* – traps a layer of warm air next to an animal's body, helping to insulate it and retain body heat in cold environments.

Reptiles lack this insulation, and have to bask in sunlight during the day (and roost at night) to maintain their body temperature. We say that they're cold-blooded, or *ectothermic* ('outside heated').

Mammals, on the other hand, are warm-blooded, or *endothermic* ('inside heated'). They produce more body heat at rest, and maintain their body temperature at roughly the same level all day (and night) long. Having a hairy or furry coat (along with more layers of body fat) helps mammals to do this by insulating them.

So their warm blood, extra fat and insulating coats

allowed mammals to do lots of things reptiles couldn't. Like hunt at night while most reptiles were curled up, motionless, to conserve energy. Or spread into colder, cloudier regions of the world – like the Arctic, Antarctica and high mountaintops – where cold-blooded reptiles simply could not survive.

And that's why there are polar bears and Arctic foxes, but no snow snakes or ice lizards?
Exactly. We warm, hairy, milky mammals can chill out in places where reptiles would only chill to death.

Yeah, but if we could make our own *milkshakes*, then we'd *really* be chillin'.
Well, we can. We just have to use electric blenders to do it. Sadly, we're unlikely to evolve the ability to produce milkshakes, since we can happily survive without them.

I can't!
Fine. Go make one with a blender, then. See? Mammals *can* make milkshakes!

Marsupial crossword

Across

1 Looks like a cross between a beaver and a mallard

Down

2 The world's largest marsupial

3 Like a wee kangaroo

4 Toothy, long-extinct beast whose Latin name was Tylacoleo Carnifex

5 Eucalyptus-loving tree-climber, often mistaken for a bear

6 The only marsupial native to North America

(answers on page 209)

How big does a whale baby get?

The largest, a blue whale calf, can be 8 m (24 feet) in length at birth, and weigh over three tonnes – or roughly the same size and weight as a large transit van. The adult blue whale is not only the largest animal on the planet, it may also be the largest animal that ever lived.

The largest animal ever? No way! Some dinosaurs must have been *way* bigger than whales.

Nope. The biggest, heaviest known dinosaurs were the sauropods, and among them *Brachiosaurus* was the largest. A full-grown *Brachiosaurus* measured up to 25 m (80 feet) long, and weighed in at less than 90 tonnes. By contrast, the *average* female blue whale is 10 feet longer and 30 tonnes heavier, at 26 m (90 feet) long and 120 tonnes.

Whoa. That is pretty heavy.
That's nothing. The *largest* blue whale on record was 30 m (100 feet) long, and weighed almost *200* tonnes. That's almost twice as much as a *Brachiosaurus.*

So how did they get so big? Whales, I mean, not dinosaurs. Although those too, I suppose . . .
Both probably evolved their enormous bulk as a defence against predators. Basically, the larger you are, the fewer predators you're likely to have. There were too many things that could take on a *Brachiosaurus*

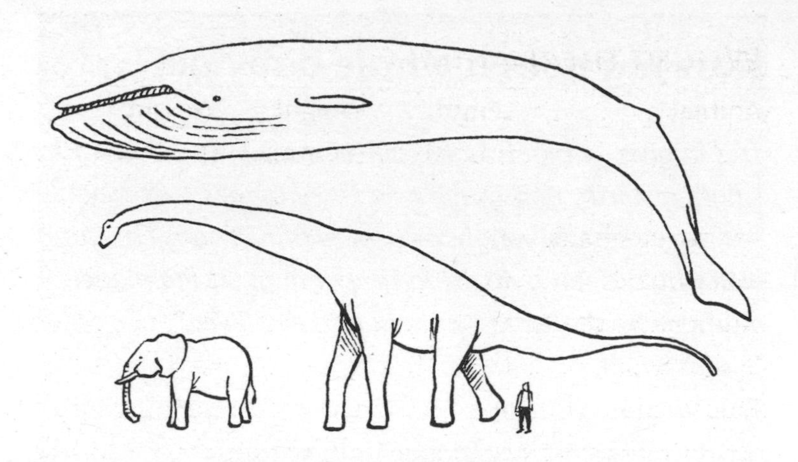

in the prehistoric world. Nor are there many things around today (besides humans) that can kill a large whale. But while most land animals are limited in size by the amount of body weight they can support and shift with their legs, whales take advantage of their salt-water home to support their huge bodies.

How do they do that?

By *floating*. Although incredibly heavy, a whale's body is still *buoyant*, meaning it can displace enough water to float, and only dives when it wants to. So using the water to support their weight has allowed whales to grow larger than they could have on land. And while the largest land animals, African bush elephants, stand up to 4 m (12 feet) tall and weigh 4–7 tonnes, many whales reach *considerably* larger sizes. Check out the list opposite.

Weight there animal

Animal	Length (in metres)	Weight (in tonnes)	Weight (in elephants)
African elephant	4	5	1
Killer whale	10	10	2
Humpback whale	14	40	8
Sperm whale	18	45	9
Blue whale	26	120	24

So, many whales are *many times* larger than even the largest of land animals. But they weren't always that big. In fact, they *couldn't* get that big until after they'd made their way back to the sea.

***Back* to the sea?**

Right. Back. Because whales – as you know – are mammals. And, like all other mammals, they descended from fish and amphibians that left the water to make their lives on land. There, their ancestors evolved legs, lungs, warm blood, fur and mammary glands. Only later did they walk back into swamps and shallow seas, lose their legs and evolve back into aquatic animals. The whole journey from sea to land and back again took over 300 million years. But by the Tertiary era, around 15 million years after the extinction of most dinosaurs, early whales were happily swimming the prehistoric oceans.

Whales had legs once? Weird. What did they look like?

Whales, dolphins and porpoises form the family of animals known as cetaceans, whose closest *living* relatives on land are probably hippos.* But their earliest known ancestors are from the group **archaeoceti** (or 'the ancient whales'), which lived in freshwater rivers and swamps over 50 million years ago. They had four stubby (but working) legs, and probably trotted between the land and water while hunting, breeding and avoiding large predators. But in their hind leg, the thigh (or femur) bone grew smaller, and they were already starting to look more streamlined and whale-like. *Ambulocetus* ('walking whale'), another ancient whale ancestor, was about the size of a modern sea lion, and probably moved in much the same way. In the water, it would ripple its spine to swim, with its webbed feet trailing behind it, while on land it would walk with its front limbs, dragging its weaker hind limbs behind it.

Of these two, modern-day whales and dolphins probably evolved from **archaeoceti**, eventually losing their hind limbs altogether and evolving flukes (or fins) on the ends of their tails that would propel them through the water. Their nostrils also moved to the tops of their heads, forming a blow-hole through

---

* For more about this, see 'How fast can a wild horse hoof it?' on page 177.

which the whale could breathe without lifting its whole head out of the water.

Crazy. But how do we *know* all this stuff?

Mostly from fossil evidence. We've actually found complete, fossilized skeletons of archaeocetes and other 'missing links' – complete with half-formed legs – all around the world. The skeleton of the oldest known cetacean, *Pakicetus*, was found in Pakistan in the early 1990s, and helped to solve some of the mysteries of how whales and dolphins evolved. Fossils like these also confirm Darwin's theory of evolution in general. As do *living* whales, if you look closely enough.

How's that, then?

Well, whale bodies are – frankly – far from perfectly designed or engineered, as aquatic animals go. They're clearly the imperfect result of natural selection working with the 'tools' and 'material' it had available.

Whales, for example, can't breathe underwater. They have to come to the surface to breathe, losing them valuable hunting time, and putting them at the constant risk of drowning. They've evolved to become more efficient at this surface-breathing, as their nostrils moved to the tops of their heads to form a blowhole. But it's still not as efficient as simply having gills – as fish do – to extract oxygen from the water directly.

So why didn't they just, you know, re-evolve those?
Because whilst evolving into mammals, the gill bones were already repurposed to make jawbones and inner ears.* So evolution didn't have the right materials to work with, and had to come up with a 'bodge job' – or a 'good enough' design, rather than a perfect one.

Similarly, although early whales probably moved *well enough* in the water, they still weren't as speedy and agile as most fish – including those they *wanted to eat* and the big ones – like sharks – that *wanted to eat them*. So instead of re-evolving fish-like bodies and movements – which would have been difficult or impossible to do – natural selection came up with alternative solutions that would allow the cetaceans to survive in the water.

Like what?
Some, like blue whales, just got *huge*, which deterred most predators. Those same animals solved the fish-chasing problem by eating plankton instead – evolving net-like baleen teeth to filter the water and catch over a *tonne* of krill each day.

---

* More about this on page 120.

Some, like dolphins and porpoises, evolved their own ways of swimming, with up-and-down tail motions that proved just as fast as (or sometimes faster than) the side-to-side thrashing of sharks and tuna. Others, like sperm whales and killer whales, evolved to become truly ferocious instead. Sperm whales actually eat sharks and giant squid, while killer whales prey on other mammals, including seals, porpoises and even (far larger) whales.

But perhaps the most impressive thing cetaceans evolved was *intelligence*. Humpback whales migrate tens of thousands of miles across the world's oceans, using rumbling, infrasonic whalesong to talk to each other over distances of 2,000 miles (3,000 km) or more.

Dolphins, meanwhile, hunt fish in packs – communicating with each other using rapid ultrasonic clicks. In tests, dolphins have shown true problem-solving intelligence, and can recognize their own images in mirrors or video displays. And they're well known for their playful, curious natures – often playing with swimmers or divers for hours on end.

Really? I wanna play! Where can I swim with a dolphin, or spot a whale out at sea?

For now, lots of places. But unless we protect them from being struck by ships, caught in fishing nets or harpooned by whaling fleets, they won't be around forever. Many species of whale and dolphin are

already endangered, and one – the Chinese river dolphin – went extinct just a few years ago.

Wow. They spend 300 million years surviving the land and sea, and then we come along with a big fishing boat. Doesn't seem fair.

It's not. And that's exactly why we need to look after them. After all – they're graceful, they're playful, they're intelligent and – above all else – they're *family*. We clever mammals have got to look out for our own, as some of us aren't as smart as we should be.

Aqua-mammal anagrams

Unravel these anagrams, and reveal eight different species of cetacean mammal.

Rise poop
Garth while
Law hub eel
Maple shrew
Warlike hell
Bootes lent hold pin
Lawn rah
Pinch mold moon

(*answers on page 209*)

How fast can a wild horse hoof it?

No one knows for sure. A thoroughbred racehorse can manage up to 43 mph (70 km per hour) over short distances, and that's carrying a human jockey. Without that extra weight – and driven by survival, rather than whipping – a wild mustang can probably go at least 5–10 mph faster. In both cases, horses owe their speed not to jockeys or predators, but to their hoofed feet.

You really think a wild horse would be faster? But aren't racehorses, like, *bred* to run fast?

That's true, they are. It's a form of *artificial selection* which has been going on for over a thousand years, or ever since humans started taming and breeding horses.

But, for tens of thousands of years before that, natural selection was already weeding out the quick from the slow, as anyone who has ever seen a pack of wild mustangs run will clearly see. They can hold a speed of 37 mph (60 km per hour) for several miles – far faster than a racehorse could manage over the same distance. And with no rider to weigh them down they could probably outrun even a champion thoroughbred if they had to.*

---

* Although if they were both weighed down with riders, then it might be a different story. Place your bets now!

Okay . . . but why do hoofs make such a difference to how fast a horse can run? Aren't they just like the tyres on a racing car?

More like the tyres, the wheels and a good part of the engine. Hoofs do more than just grip the ground and stop the horse's feet from getting blisters when it runs. In fact, evolving hoofs has reshaped the entire horse's leg, and provided the driving force that has taken them to top speed.

How's that, then? And what exactly are hoofs, anyway?

Hoofs are basically cylindrical, wrap-around finger-nails or toenails.They're made of the same stuff as human nails and tiger claws – interlocked fibres of the hard protein keratin. But unlike fingernails and claws, hoofs have evolved to bear weight. In fact, in many hoofed animals, they support the *entire weight* of the legs and body above.

So horses are standing on their toenails?

Right. And if you're not impressed by that, *you* try doing it some time. It's easy enough to stand on your tiptoes, and with special shoes ballet dancers can stand on the very tips of them for several minutes at a time. But even the best ballerina in the world can't stand on her toe*nails* for more than a second . . . much less *run* and *jump* on them.

Horses can do this because the *whole shape of the legs* has altered along with the toes. To get some idea of how much they've been altered, try this.

Look down at the bones of your hands and feet. Not the fingers and toes – just the hand and foot bones. Now imagine what they would look like if they were stretched out until they were almost the same length as your forearms and shin bones. Extend your middle fingers (check the room first to make sure you're not going to offend anyone), curl all the others into your palm and imagine that middle finger (including the fingernail) was as wide as your whole hand.

Urrrrgh. Weird.

Right. But that, basically, is what has happened to horses – and many other hoofed mammals – over evolutionary time. The bones of the horse's 'hands' and 'feet' (the metacarpal and metatarsal bones) have stretched to almost the same length as their 'forearm' and 'shin' bones. Their middle fingers and toes have expanded, and all the other fingers and toes disappeared completely. In other ungulates, different numbers of 'fingers' or 'toes' may remain, but horses, zebras and their relatives have just one, because this works to their speedy advantage.

But why would that have happened? What good does it do?

Evolving longer 'feet' and single-digit hoofs does two main things. First, it gives the horse a longer stride, so it covers more ground with each running step. Second, it creates more joints that can flex outwards – as opposed to our finger-joints, which only really flex inwards,* towards the palm. This gives the horse more power in its stride, and so increases the number of strides a horse can make per minute (the stride rate). These two features combine to make the horse a super-speedy running machine. One that, oddly, runs on its toenails.

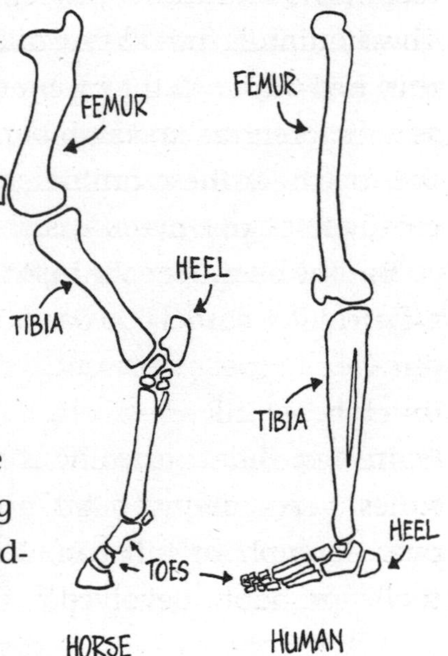

* Unless, of course, your older brother is viciously bending them that way. In any case, they're not *supposed* to bend backwards.

But speed isn't the only (or even the main) reason why so many hoofed animals have evolved. Horses are just one of over 250 species of hoofed mammals (or *ungulates*), many of which evolved hoofs for very different reasons.

Traditionally, ungulates have been split into two major groups or orders – those with an odd number of toes (the Perissodactyla) and those with an even number of toes (the Artiodactyla).

The odd-toed Perissodactyla include one-toed horses and zebras (Family Equidae), but also three-toed rhinos (Rhinocerotidae) and tapirs* (Tapiridae). These animals are all fast runners – an African black rhinoceros can hit 32 mph at full charge, and tapirs can hit similar speeds over small bursts through the forest. So these animals probably evolved hoofs chiefly to escape predators.

But the even-toed Artiodactyla include animals as different as camels, cows, giraffes, hippos, deer and antelope. While deer, antelope, gazelles and giraffes (yep – they can hit over 35 mph at full run too!) probably evolved

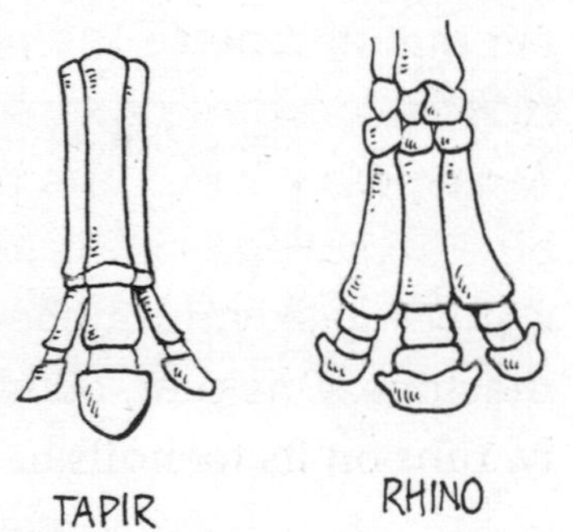

* **Tapirs** live in the jungles of Malaysia and Brazil. They have three toes on each back foot, but four on the front. They swim very well, and when they do so they like to use their long, flexible noses as snorkels!

their hoofs for speed too, others evolved them for different reasons.

Okay – like what?

Camels, buffalo, bison and cattle probably evolved them to protect their feet. This gave them the extra endurance they needed to survive long migrations over the plains and deserts of Africa, Asia and North America, in search of new lands for grazing.

Others, such as mountain goats, bighorn sheep and yak (a long-haired, cow-like animal that lives throughout the Himalayas) may have evolved them primarily for grip – allowing them to stay sure-footed whilst making their escapes on rocky mountain crags. And still others, like domestic sheep and cows, may simply have had ancestors with hoofs once, but no longer really need them now.

In any case, hoofs have helped ungulate mammals to replace the dinosaurs as the most widespread and numerous herbivores on the planet. Where once huge *Iguanadons* and *Brachiosauruses* chewed their way through the Earth's plant life, millions of sheep, cattle, bison, wildebeest, reindeer, elk and antelope now trim the trees, bushes and grasses in their place.

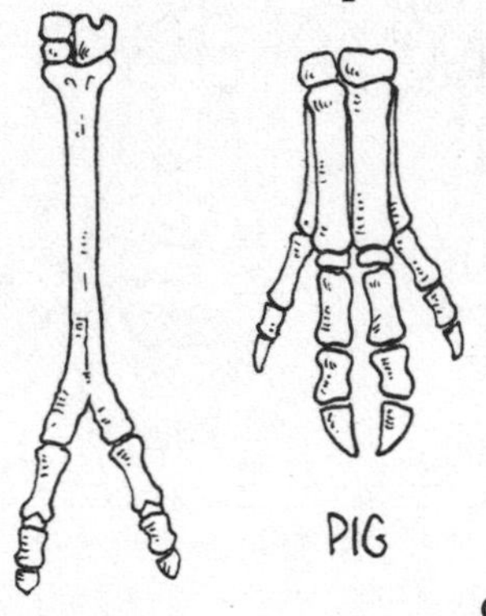

Wow. Never thought of it like that.
Bet you'll never look at a sheep the same way again, eh?

Hmm. Bet you a fiver a racehorse could still beat a mustang, though . . .
Oh, *give* over.

Hidden hoofs wordsearch

How many hidden hoofed mammals can you find?

Wildebeest	Zebra	Tapir	Antelope
Rhinoceros	Ibex	Dikdik	Horse
Yak	Bison	Okapi	Giraffe

Bighorn sheep (separate words in puzzle)

```
C Z I H A X J A A L M K W S E
T Q J H Y R R W L T R T K O M
D Q A X Y A B S Q S C R K R M
A N T E L O P E D U Y X O E D
E S R O H D K I Z T P Y G C U
X Z V S P G K A S P A K I O M
A L W E N D W E P K E X R N U
A B E J I D E Z B I L W A I Z
P H K K B B P C N I Y F F H R
S X R D E B I S O N G Z F R I
S B S D X K M Y S T R H E C P
Q C L G J R O K Q E Q V O R A
K I A U S Q M H W J B L Z R T
W V Q Z S U N I X N K R F C N
Q H R X Q H E L N K J E H H Q
```

(answers on page 210)

Are bats really vampires?

If you mean 'are they really bloodsucking monsters that turn into trendy, good-looking humanoids and back again?', then no – they aren't. But if you mean 'are they really blood-drinkers?', then yes – a few of them are. But only a few. Most other bats prefer insects, frogs, fish or fresh fruit. Honest.

Wait a second – you're telling me bloodsucking vampire bats are real?
Yes, but . . .

Yaaggghhh! Then where are they? Are they coming to get me?
Okay, fine – let's get this over with. Yes, vampire bats do exist. But, no, they're not coming to get you.

How d-d-do y-y-you kn-n-n-ow? They c-c-could be!
Look – calm down. For starters, they live in Central and South America, so unless you're reading this book on holiday in the Americas, you're fine. And although some vampire bats feed on mammalian blood,* they much prefer pigs, horses and cattle to people.

* Others feed on birds – mostly chickens and turkeys on farms.

Urrrrrgh! So they do it? Do they, like, swoop down and bite their necks?

Well, while a few will hang from horses' manes as they feed, most usually begin their 'attacks' from the ground, and so most often go for a leg or flank. Vampires are unique among bats in that they move very well on the ground. Most bats can't take off from the ground, so prefer to land in trees or on vertical surfaces between flights. (This is also why they sleep hanging upside down from cave or attic ceilings, instead of curled up on the floor.)

Vampires, however, can leap from the ground into a vertical take-off, and creep and crawl very quickly on flat ground. So to avoid being seen by their victims, they usually land a metre or so behind them, then creep up and clamber up their legs. Once there, they use their razor-sharp fangs to stealthily and painlessly shave off a flap of skin. Vampire bat saliva contains a chemical called an anticoagulant, which stops blood from clotting. So the animal's blood begins to flow freely from the small wound, with the victim unaware that it has even been bitten.

That still gives me the creeps. In fact, that may be even worse than a full-on neck bite. Okay – so what happens then? They drain all the animal's blood and kill it, right?

Wrong. They lap away with their tongues just like a cat laps up water or milk (vampire bats do not suck

blood!) for up to twenty minutes, but rarely take more than a couple of teaspoonfuls of blood at a time (their stomachs can't expand to take any more than that and, besides, if they lapped up too much blood and became too heavy they'd never take off and fly away). That said, they do sometimes return to the same victim, night after night, to get more.

Yuck! Bats are EVIL! I'm glad there are none of those round here.

Bats aren't evil. Even vampire bats are just doing what they evolved to do – exploiting a nutritious food source instead of chasing more mobile prey. Besides, there are only three species of vampire bat in the world out of over 1,000.

Bats help us? I don't believe you.

It's true, they do. Together, a colony of insect-eating bats will munch tens of millions of pesky mosquitoes and midges in one night, amongst other buggy prey. Without them, people in warmer climes would suffer a lot more mosquito bites (and mosquito-borne diseases like malaria).

They eat bugs? What else do they eat?

That depends on the species. There are bats that hunt frogs, bats that pluck fish from rivers and lakes, even vegetarian bats that eat nuts, figs, dates, peaches, mangoes and bananas! In fact, many of these species

are important for fruit-growers, as they pollinate fruit trees in much the same way as bees pollinate flowers.

Vegetarian bee-bats? They don't sound so bad . . .
Actually, fruit bats may be among the scariest-*looking* bats in the world, if only because of their size. The largest of them has a wingspan of over 1.6m (or 5.5 feet). That's probably as wide as you are tall!

But most bats are *much* smaller – with an average body length of 7–8 cm (3–4 inches) and a wingspan of 15–30 cm (6–12 inches).

Yeah, but those bat wings are scary. They're all thin and leathery and . . . ugh! What are they made of, anyway?
Bat wings are basically big flaps of skin stretched between their fingers. They're very different from bird wings, which are made of rows of specialized hairy vanes (or feathers) that project backwards from the bird's lower and upper arms.

Evolving along a separate mammalian path, bats developed wings in a different way – from flaps of skin (like on the webbed feet of frogs and ducks) between their extended fingers.* They may have originally used these to 'net' insects. But over time their fingers extended and the area of the finger-flaps expanded.

---

* The scientific name for the order of bats, Chiroptera, means 'hand-wing' in Greek.

This gave bats the ability to glide from treetops, and then flap to stay in the air for longer. And although they might not be as fast and powerful as bird wings, these bat 'finger-wings' are very finely controllable, making the bat extremely agile in the air. Most bats can fly in complete darkness, turning and dropping suddenly in mid-flight in order to catch moths and other bugs on the wing.

How do they do that? I heard they were blind, but they use radar or something.

Close. Bats aren't actually blind – many just don't have great eyesight,* as they're **nocturnal** animals (meaning they're most active at night), and eyesight isn't much help in total darkness. So instead they evolved a form of *sonar* (rather than radar) – which is a way of picturing the pitch-black world around them using high-pitched sounds and **echolocation**.

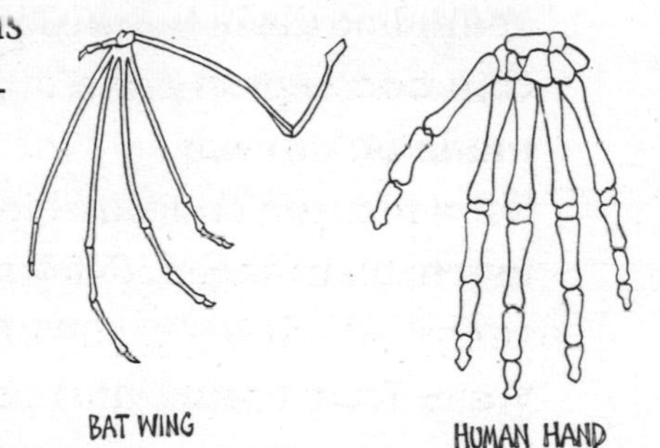

The basic idea is similar to the game Marco Polo, in which the blindfolded 'hunter' keeps calling out the word 'Marco', and the other players shout back

* The exceptions to this are some fruit bats, which are active during the day, and have pretty good eyesight, thank you very much.

'Polo'. Eventually, the hunter follows the sound all the way to his 'prey', and reaches out to nab them.

Well, now imagine the hunters are bats, and the players are moths. The bats call out with rapid clicking sounds, which are ultrasonic – meaning that they're so high-pitched that the human ear can't hear them. The clicks echo off objects around the bats – including moths – and from the time it takes to return to the bat's ears, its brain can quickly calculate not only which direction it's in, but also how far away it is.

The bat releases three to five clicks per second until it locates a moth, and then increases the number of echoing clicks (up to 200 per second or more) as it draws closer to its prey. At this rate, it can 'see' the entire world immediately around it as a high-definition 'sound-scape'. And it can zero in on the movement of a tiny moth or mosquito from over 20 m (60 feet) away.

Wow. That's brilliant. Those moths are *done for*.

Many are – a single bat may catch over 100 moths per night this way, and an entire colony (of up to three million bats in some places!) will consume millions of them. But some moths actually fight back with sonic weapons of their own. As the bat approaches, furiously clicking away and listening for its tell-tale echoes, these moths will SCREAM in ultrasound at the last minute, temporarily deafening the bat. Or, at the very least, leaving it unable to tell where the echoes are coming from.

Cool! Still – wouldn't want to be that moth.

Me neither. But if you want to get an idea of what it would feel like, try one of these games with your friends!

Be a bat!

Echolocation for beginners

Try these bat-based variations on the game Marco Polo (see opposite).

Basic:

Everyone blindfolded; one player (the 'bat') shouts 'EEEEEEEEEK!', while the others (the 'moths') shout 'AGGHHHHH!' in response, until the bat closes in on one and grabs him/her/it.

Realistic:

As above, but all are armed with those dog-training clickers, which you can buy cheaply from most pet shops. The 'bat' clicks three times per second; the moths click back. Speed up the number of clicks as the bat gets louder (and therefore closer).

Fun:

Everyone blindfolded, outside; the 'bat' has a water pistol, and shoots at random; 'moths' scream when they get hit. 'Bat' closes in for a super-soaking.

Do tigers purr?

No. At least not like your pet cat does. Tigers and other big cats have different bone structures in their throats to smaller cats. So while tigers, lions and leopards can make rumbling noises in their throats, they can only do it while breathing out – not continuously like your house-kitty can. On the other hand, almost all big cats can roar, which is a far more useful noise for life in the wild.

So big cats don't really purr? Why not?

Because although they're all in the same family of mammals, the *Felidae*, and they all share common ancestors, big cats and domestic cats have evolved different 'voices' – each suited to their lifestyles. And big cats, it seems, may have traded in their ability to make a constant prrrrrrrrrrrrrrrrrr, prrrrrrrrrrrr in favour of a much louder (and scarier) RRWWWWW-WWWWRRRRRRRRR!

How did that happen?

Well, domestic cats and other small cats (of the genus *Felis*) have a solid hyoid bone in their throats, which supports their tongue and vocal muscles. As air flows back and forth across this bone with each inhale and exhale, the hyoid (along with the vocal muscles) vibrate, creating a continuous prrrrrrrrrrr sound. Cats, as you may have gathered, use purring for communication.

Like, to tell you they're happy?
Amongst other things, yes. But different pitches of purr – from a deep rumble to a high trill – can also mean different things, such as 'I'm nervous', 'I'm angry' or even 'I'm in pain'.

Oh. I didn't know that. So if tigers can't purr, how are you supposed to know if they're happy, nervous, angry or what?
Well, frankly, even if they could purr, would you want to risk getting close enough to listen?

Er . . . no. Good point.
Right. And nor would most animals. Including other tigers. Which may be one reason why big cats have evolved a more long-distance alternative. In most big cats (of the genus *Panthera*), the hyoid bone has elastic sections that can slide and stretch like a trombone as exhaled air blasts its way past. On the downside, this doesn't provide enough solid support for a continuous purr. On the upside, it does (along with the vocal muscles) allow them to create a faster, harder, louder vibration, otherwise known as a ROAR!

And they use that to scare off other cats, right?
Right. Big cats can roar out warnings at a distance of 5 miles (8 km) or more. But, as smaller cats do with purrs, they also use roars closer up to attract mates, or express anger, nervousness or pain.

So while small cats can purr but not roar, most big cats can roar but not purr. Similarly, while dogs (Canidae) and bears (Ursidae) are quite closely related, dogs can bark but not roar while bears can roar but not bark.

Dogs and bears are related?
Yep. In fact, dogs, bears and cats are all part of a larger order of mammals called Carnivora.

Which means 'meat-eaters', right?
Right. But while the word *carnivore* means 'anything that eats meat' (and so includes many reptiles, birds, and even one or two plants!), Carnivora refers

only to eleven or so families of **mostly meat-eating mammals**. (Triple 'Ms', if you like!) Many biologists, though, use these two words interchangeably. So we will too.

Hang on – *mostly* meat-eating? Don't they *all* eat meat?

Well, all carnivores have evolved special adaptations to hunting and scavenging freshly killed prey. But that doesn't mean they always kill it themselves, nor that they *always* eat meat. Some, like hyenas and raccoons, are mostly scavengers, rather than hunters. And others – like pandas and aardwolves – feed on plants, fish, insects or a mixture of these. But even those species that *don't* hunt or eat meat usually still look like they *could* if they wanted to . . .

How's that?

For starters, all carnivores have powerful jaws and special, blade-like teeth called **carnassids** (also known as canines) that are adapted for slicing and tearing off chunks of raw flesh. Many also have pointed claws for a similar purpose. To back up these fearsome weapons, they also have strong bones and flexible joints (where our wrists and ankles would be) that give them the ability to run, jump, climb and pounce on their fleeing prey. They also typically have just one litter of young per year, have five toes on each front foot, and four or five on each rear foot.

How many kinds of carnivore are there?
If we're talking Carnivora, there are about 270 species, arranged into 11 families. These include:

- Felidae (domestic cats, wild cats, jungle cats, lions, tigers, leopards, jaguars, panthers, pumas)
- Canidae (dogs, wolves, dingoes)
- Hyaenadae (hyenas, aardwolves)
- Ursidae (bears)
- Procyonidae (raccoons, kinkajous)
- Mustelidae (weasels, minks, skunks, otters)
- Herpestidae (mongooses, meerkats)
- Viverridae (civets, genets, binturongs)

Many of these you may never have heard of. Civets and genets, for example, look like large, dog-sized weasels or meerkats, and live throughout Africa and South-east Asia. Binturongs (otherwise known as bear-cats) look like massive all-black racoons with long, muscular tails.* They, too, live in the forests of South-east Asia. Though you don't hear about (or see) them much, civets, genets and binturongs may well be closest in appearance to miacids, the first mammalian carnivores, which evolved a few million years after most of the dinosaurs copped it at the end of the Cretaceous period. From these strange animals, all

* Which they use to grip trees and hang upside down from tree branches. They also, strangely, smell like popcorn.

modern cats, dogs, bears and other Carnivora have since evolved and spread around the world.

Cool! But I want to see them. I've never seen half of those animals – except for cats and dogs, that is. If there are so many of these cool, furry carnivores out there, then where are they all hiding?

Many – like raccoons – are nocturnal, meaning that they only come out at night. Others – like bears – are solitary, unsociable animals that stay hidden from humans wherever possible. And, sadly, many of the largest mammalian carnivores are rare or endangered.

Why's that? If they're so big and fearsome, shouldn't there be loads of them around? You know, ruling the food chains, like *The Lion King* or something?

If it wasn't for their main rivals – us – there probably would be. The simple fact is that large carnivores need large amounts of prey to live on, and large habitats to live in. And both of these have been steadily decreasing for thousands of years, thanks to human poaching and settlement. In South America's rainforests, jaguars and many smaller species of wild cat are threatened by forest burning to create new farmland. In the mountains of North America, Northern Europe and Asia, many bears face threats from hunting and

logging. And in China and India, pandas and tigers are critically endangered thanks to forest destruction to create new homes, and poachers looking for pelts and body parts for exotic (and useless) medicines.

That's terrible. So what do we do?

Join efforts to protect them, preserve the habitats of the animals that are left and find ways to live alongside them. Carnivores can be scary animals, but so can we humans. The sooner we realize that it isn't 'them or us', the sooner we can learn to coexist on this planet, as we already have for many thousands of years.

That way, we can all get to hear tiger roars – along with cat purrs – for many years to come.

Are human beings animals, apes or just people?

We're all three! Like all other mammal species, we humans are hairy, warm-blooded, give birth to live young and nurse them with self-made milk. Like all other primates (which includes both apes and monkeys), humans have keen vision, forward-facing eyes and thumb joints that let us grip things. And although we've lost much of our hair and fur, and our brains have some extra bits, we're more similar to our distant mammal cousins than we sometimes like to think.

Oh, come on. There are *loads* of things that make us different from apes and monkeys. We're *nothing like* them.

Okay . . . like what kinds of things?

Well, their bodies are all hairy. All over.

True, but up until quite recently, so were we. Some of our hominid (or human-like) ancestors, like *Australopithecus*, were every bit as hairy as any ape or monkey. It's only been 5 million years since they walked the plains of Africa. And even now we are still hairy animals. Especially as adult males. It's just that the hair has become thinner and lighter – only remaining thick and heavy in certain places on the body, like the head, face, armpits and groin.

All right, then – what about walking? And talking? And using tools? And we're *much* cleverer.
That's true, we are cleverer. And no other primate can talk, either. But we're actually not the only ones that can walk on two legs. Nor are we the only primates that use tools. It's just that we do these things *a lot better* than the others.

Really? There are walking and tool-using apes out there somewhere? Other than us, I mean.
Yes – there really are. And, if you think about it, it makes perfect sense. After all, we already know that at the end of the Cretaceous period, the only mammals on the planet were little shrew-like animals scampering at the feet of the ailing dinosaurs. Yet here we are today, 65 million years later, as walking, talking, tool-using, super-smart mammals. Therefore, we *had* to have evolved these features and abilities at some point in between. And if you follow the history of the primates, by looking at the families still with us today, you can see how it all happened.

So how did it happen?
Thought you'd never ask . . .

It all began about 65 million years ago, with those little four-legged scampering, shrew-mammals. Some of them evolved into the weasel-like miacids, which eventually led to the carnivores. Others evolved into the hoofed ungulates, toothy rodents and rabbits,

flippered dolphins and whales and flapping bats.

But one group took to the trees, evolving longer limbs and grasping hands to help them leap and climb between lofty branches. These animals would have looked a lot like today's **prosimians** (meaning 'before-monkeys'), which include lemurs, lorises and bushbabies. Animals like this were the very first primates. Like us, they have opposable (or backward-facing) thumbs, which means they can grip tree branches and hold pieces of fruit while they eat them.

Big deal. So can squirrels.
Squirrels don't eat fruit.

You know what I mean.
Okay, fine. If you're not impressed by that, then get this. Lemurs and lorises also have two large, forward-facing eyes, which gives them overlapping, stereoscopic vision. With these, they can accurately judge distances between branches – which obviously comes in handy if you need to jump to survive. Lemurs also,

occasionally, stand upright on two legs and skip. They can't walk – since they don't have the hip structure and muscles to support their weight one leg at a time. But when they want to make a dash over an area of grassland between trees, they stand upright (to keep an eye out above the grass for predators) and skip their way to safety, one foot landing slightly after the other.

Not bad. But that's still not walking or using tools. Nothing like it.

Right, for that we have to wait another 30 million years, for the evolution of monkeys and apes. By 35 million years ago, the ancestors of monkeys, gorillas, chimps and humans were swinging and knuckle-walking their way through the ancient forests of Africa, Asia and South America. With better-developed brains, eyes and limbs, these animals learned to use their hands in more complex ways, developing hand *dexterity*. One group of these animals eventually led to the monkeys, marmosets and gibbons – who stayed high in the trees to feed on fruits and avoid predators on the ground. But another evolved into the **hominoids** (or 'human-likes'). This family includes gorillas, chimps, orang-utans and humans.

We're in the same *family*? Not just the same, like, class or order or something?

Nope. We're a whole closer than that. Our *class* is

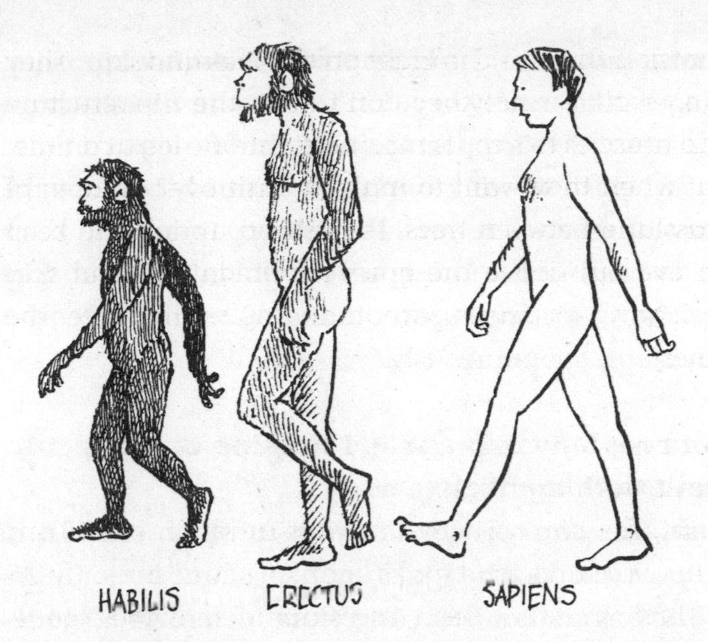

the **mammals**, our *order* the **primates**, and our *family* the **hominoids**, which we share with the other apes. Hominoids all have enlarged brains, dexterous hands and – apparently – the ability to make and use tools.

No way! What kind of tool does a chimp use?

Actually, chimps make and use lots of them, including rocks (hammers for cracking nuts), sticks and stones (weapons to ward off leopards and rivals), and thin twigs (to fish insects and grubs out of hollow trees and termite mounds). And while gorillas and orangutans aren't often seen using tools in the wild, they will use many of the same tools as chimps if given a food-related problem to solve in captivity. Which shows they have the brainpower to do it – but being bigger, and mostly vegetarian, they just rarely have the need. Gorillas, chimps and orang-utans can also easily learn to walk upright if trained. In the wild, they have stuck to knuckle-walking, since the thick underbrush of the forest prevents them from standing up. But in an open space, many will walk (at least a few steps) spontaneously.

That is pretty impressive, I suppose. But they still can't walk or talk like us.

True, they can't. There are limits to what gorillas and chimps can do. And that's because of one major thing we have that they don't – an expanded region of outer brain called the **cerebral cortex**. It's this that makes our species truly different from all the other primates – and unique among all the other mammals.

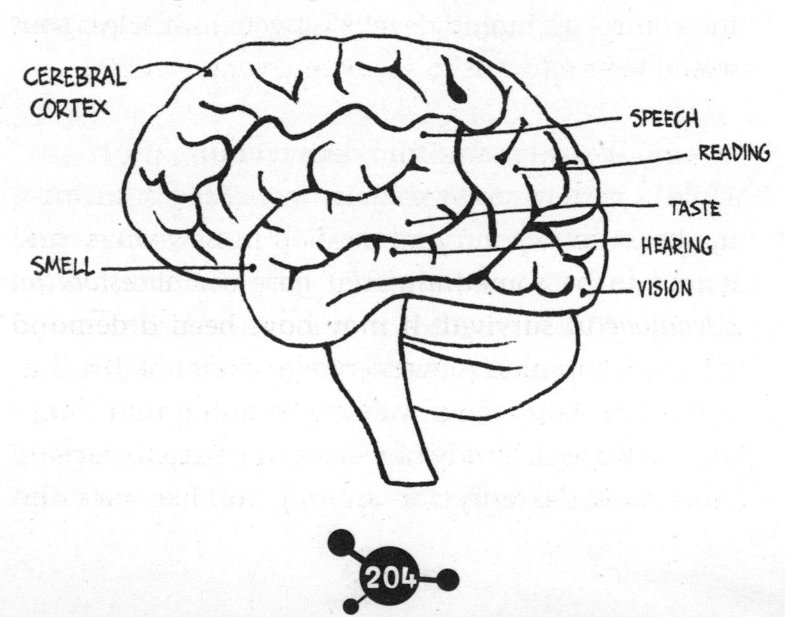

At some point, around 5 million years ago, our ancestors split off from those of chimpanzees and bonobos (pygmy chimpanzees). And when they did their brains went through a biological Big Bang. Within a few million years, we went from grunting half-intelligent apes to agile, upright, two-legged hunters with an intelligence never before seen in the history of the animal kingdom.

From early hominids like *Australopithecus* to *Homo habilis* ('handy man'), *Homo erectus* ('upright man', and finally to our own species, *Homo sapiens* ('clever man'), our brains became more and more complex. With newly-developed areas of the outer brain, and some extra rewiring throughout bits of the rest, the limits to our mental development were removed. With this, we began to develop more and more sophisticated forms of body control – including the control of highly-developed vocal muscles, that would later allow us to speak and communicate.

So what caused that Big Brainy Bang?

To be honest, we don't know for sure. *Something* drove the brain to expand and develop in new ways, and it had to be something that *gave our ancestors an advantage* in survival. It may have been a demand for more complex movements (or motor skills) that came with balancing, walking, running and jumping on two legs. It may have been the need to develop more hand dexterity, for crafting tools like axes and spear heads. It may have been the need to communicate with each other in hunting, or in teaching others how to craft weapons and tools. Later, when our brains were developed enough, we began to dance, sing and produce simple artworks – like cave paintings or carved wooden figures. At this point, perhaps females started to prefer the better dancers, singers and artists, and helped to select for bigger, more creative brains . . .

Wow – that's a big list of brainy ideas! So which was it?

Who knows? Perhaps one day soon we'll find out.

But until then we can still sit safe in the knowledge that our brains and our intelligence is what makes our species, *Homo sapiens*, truly unique. But at the same time, recognizing our similarities to the other apes helps to remind us of what we have in common.

Looking at humans alongside lemurs, monkeys, gorillas and chimps, we can plainly see that we're are all primates . . . all mammals . . . and that we're all connected.

But I hope now that you see, also, that our links with the animal kingdom go much deeper – all the way to the air sacs we share with amphibians, the backbones we share with fish, the guts we share with worms, the cells we share with sponges, and the DNA we share with the many billions of bacteria that live in and around our bodies.

All forms of life are one – one wonderful union of living things, linked to each other through our shared evolutionary past.

Now, in the present, it's up to us to study, respect and protect all forms of life, so we can continue to enjoy each other's company well into the future.

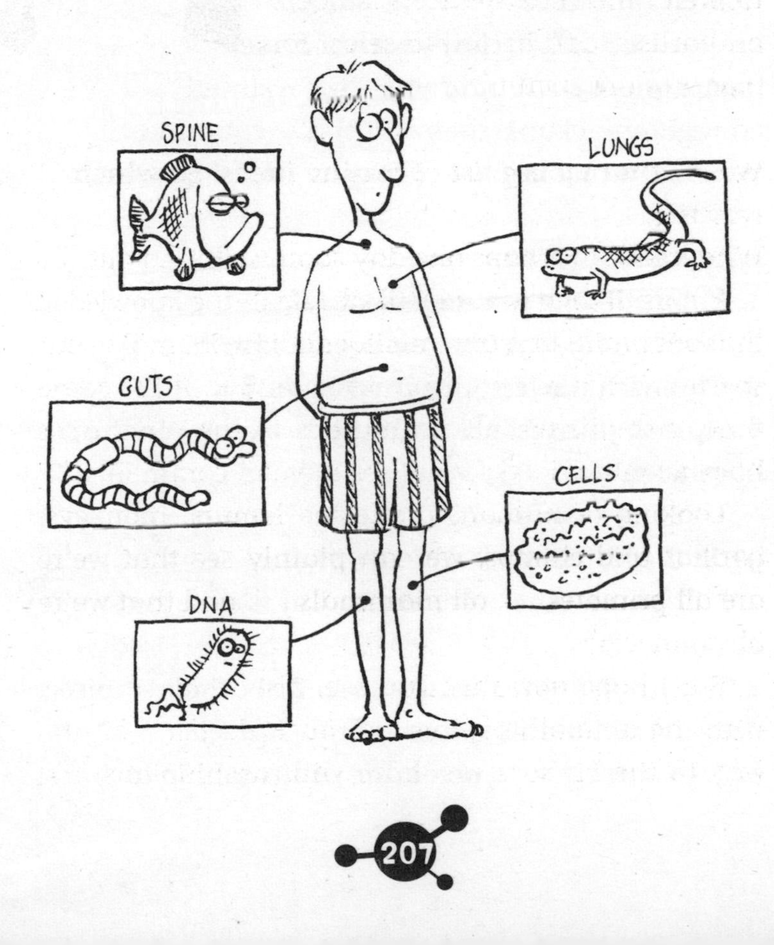

Answers

p31 Animal anagrams

Spotted skunk; killer whale; grizzly bear; red kangaroo; duck-billed platypus; giant panda

p49 Spot the hybrid

Zeedonk, liger, jaglion, yakow, zorse

p63 Fit for battle

Hyena/teeth, tiger/claws, warthog/tusks, ibex/antlers, bat/ultrasound, leaf mantis/camouflage, skunk/chemical spray, cobra/deadly venome, pangolin/body armour.

p103 Odd bug out

1. Millipede (the rest are insects)
2. Daddy long-legs (the rest are arachnids)
3. Cuttlefish (the rest are crustaceans)
4. Starfish (the rest are arthropods – yes, even the barnacle!)

p126 Bird-brainy

1 B. Elephant birds were larger, but they're no longer alive.

2 C. Some beat their wings up to 200 or more times per second, but this is rare.

3 D. In a full dive, a peregrine can reach up to

224 mph – as fast as a small aeroplane.
4 D. Roadrunners and ostriches run; penguins swim; parrots talk; cave swifts and oilbirds echolocate; crows and thrushes use tools (hooks and rock anvils) to get at grubs and snails.
And while owls can turn their heads through 270°, they can't go all the way around.

p168 Marsupial megapuzzle crossword

Across

1. Duckbilled Platypus

Down

2. Red kangaroo; 3. wallaby; 4. marsupiallion;
5. koala; 6. opossum

p176 Aqua-mammal anagrams

Porpoise
Right whale
Blue whale
Sperm whale
Killer whale
Bottlenose dolphin
Narwhal
Common dolphin

p184 Hidden Hoofs wordsearch

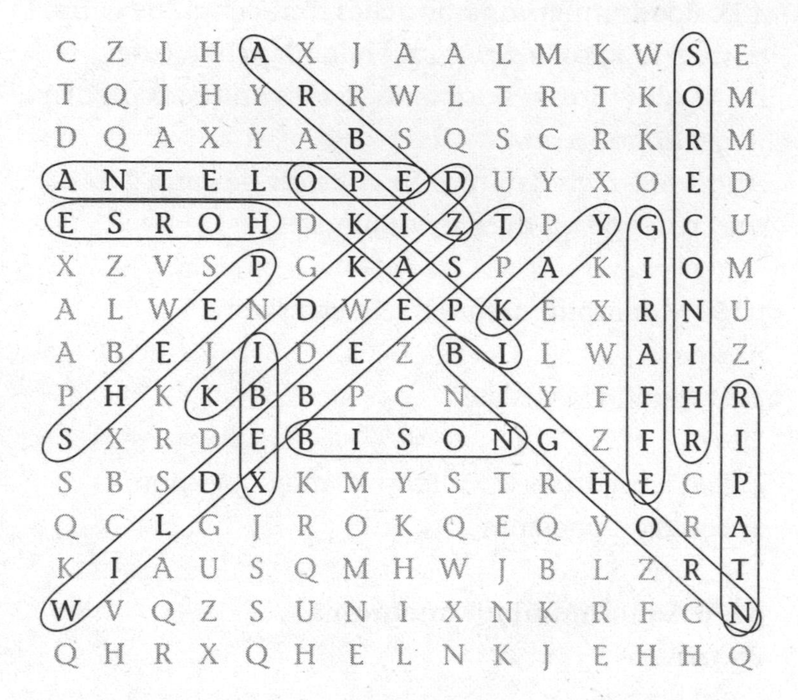

Picture Credits

Illustrations by Mike Phillips, except:

Pages 14, 15, 17, 23, 185 **Science Museum/ Science and Society Picture Library.**

SCIENCE SORTED

Space, black holes and stuff

Glenn Murphy

What is a black hole?

How do we know that stars and galaxies are billions of years old?

What is the difference between stars and planets?

Packed with information about all sorts of incredible things like supermassive black holes, galaxies, telescopes, planets, solar flares, constellations, eclipses and red dwarfs, this book has no boring bits!

Why is SNOT green?

The First Science Museum Question and Answer Book

Glenn Murphy

Why is snot green? Do rabbits fart? What is space made of? Where does all the water go at low tide? Can animals talk? What are scabs for? Will computers ever be cleverer than people?

Discover the answers to these and an awful lot of other brilliant questions frequently asked at the Science Museum in this wonderfully funny and informative book.